Dollar Planet by Peter McClard

Wealth and the End of Money

Automating Utopia

Copyright, Etc.

This book is lovingly dedicated to all of my teachers, mentors, tutors, fellow students and most especially to my family and extended family including the McClard's, the Tuz's and the Stickney's.

Table of Contents

Preface

I have no axe to grind with the "wealthy" and no political agenda to advance. This treatise is not advocating for doing away with money either, but I conclude that in an odd and possibly ironic way, it will do away with itself and no one will much care nor suffer as a consequence.

I am neither an economist nor a scientist but I did study acoustical engineering and ended up with a degree in philosophy from a school I admire called St. John's College where we read and discussed the Great Books which sparked my life as a free thinker. I also had a mildly successful run of over 20 years as an entrepreneur in the publishing software business so I know about computers and programming, which is my primary career as of writing this. I will discuss the *programmability of matter* below, a key concept. I come from a family of intellectuals who all exceeded my humble Bachelor's degree and over the years many of these topics have been discussed in one way or another and I am grateful for their role in my upbringing and life as well as so many fine people I've had the pleasure to know and discuss so much with.

Upon reading this, one may get the impression that I am a fan of robots or computers and AI and all things tech. That is not exactly so, nor am I a detractor. I didn't invent the things we see nor do I have the power to change the course of History as it has unfolded. It has a momentum to it and I am an observer who very much cares about how we proceed, if not for myself, for my children's sake and honestly, for all of humanity and creatures. That is what drives me to put these thoughts in writing. I love Nature and I love natural things so I am trying to place these technological happenings into a natural context that is in accordance with what one might call *The Good*.

This treatise is my scientific/philosophical take on the trends I see and a quest for the meaning of the terms we freely use, most specifically the meaning of *Wealth*. No shortage of fat books on the topic exist from Adam Smith's *The Wealth of Nations* to Marx's *Das Kapital* to Piketty's *Capital in the Twenty-First Century,* and some thin ones too, like *The Gospel of Wealth* by Andrew Carnegie. I have at some point in my thinking diverged drastically from these writers, drawing entirely new conclusions, though often in parallel or for similar reasons but under different, unforeseeable conditions. For example, Carnegie concludes that highly successful people in capitalism have outsmarted or out-talented others and are generally more fit in a Darwinian sense and likewise help the species survive, giving society a benefit as it "comes along for the ride." He goes further and concludes that capitalism itself is a survivor in a long line of tribal socialist and communist systems and its competitive core drives us forward by producing great wealth for the few and lifting the poor to exceed yesteryear's wealthy. While the latter part of this is undeniable, I have concluded that even capitalism is a caterpillar awaiting metamorphosis into a butterfly and it will be fully subsumed by something more advanced, pleasing and natural.

I don't deny that material wealth exists or that some people are what we call wealthy and have earned it. I seek herein to clarify and refine what it is we call wealth and to show how much the definition shifts over time and has numerous contexts with which to define it. I suppose my conclusions are somewhat radical but they are based on reason and taking trends to their logical conclusions. I don't have an exact timeline on many of these things but when it comes to seeking Truth, timelines can be stretched out and extrapolated from the Historical facts. In the end, I think I wish to show, with a different perspective, that we are in fact *all* wealthy by way of extreme overabundance. There is no material need that is technically out of reach for anybody. So this is not about Communism, Socialism, Capitalism or any other *ism* but rather about meaning, purpose and physical reality we can clearly see and hopefully agree on.

The 21st Century will show us a lot about our future as a species. Here we are near the beginning and there are already robots doing backflips, speaking to reporters, acting as human concierges, Watson winning Jeopardy and AI mastering games like Chess and Go. One can only imagine what these capabilities will be in 10, 20 or 50 years, let alone in 2100.

The Future is coming faster each day and we are entering the Age of Automation and Artificial Intelligence quite rapidly. How we will deal with the many conundrums of this new reality is entirely up for grabs and it can go many ways, with outcomes from dystopia to utopia. But I can say with certainty, we will find ourselves with new ethical challenges, new questions about our roles in life and our purpose. There is no stopping the wheels of progress or the human imagination. Therefore I am rolling with it and thinking through the consequences of that progress so that we might be able to better govern ourselves, live peacefully and with a *very* high standard of living for *Everybody*.

I will, from time to time, make predictions about the Future. These will be in the form of statements based on what I conclude would be absurd to be otherwise, given the other mitigating circumstances. In that sense, I gladly admit that much of what I am conjecturing is *theoretical* but I don't believe it's a theory. This is not a cohesive theory that can be tested but rather a set of inferences from existing trends and writings. Nor is there a particular outcome I am rooting for in what I say but rather I am trying to decipher the path we are on as a species and the various possible outcomes that could occur.

At times, I will ponder consequences of this or that event or process unfolding such as all of the cascading consequences of money becoming obsolete. How does this happen and what would it mean if it did? A simple thing like this leads to a huge pile of questions that can only be answered by future generations who may live through some of these things. So in that sense, I hope to give some insights into how we can think about these things and perhaps construct meaningful solutions to many intractable problems facing humanity.

I freely use the terms *imaginative* or *imaginary* to indicate a tenuous subject conjured up in the neurons of the imaginer or passed on to another in the form of a story. Often what I mean to indicate is the thing is *subjective* or *relative* and subject to many interpretations and can't be easily traced to *objective* or *concrete* reality, if at all.

When I use the term *AI* I don't necessarily mean "artificial intelligence," its original meaning (due to the fact that it's not of a biological nature) and arose from a branch computer science having to do with Algorithms, Data, Neural Networks and Machine Learning (ML). There are many variants such as Extended Intelligence (XI), Enhanced or Augmented Intelligence and others, and the methods of machine learning have even branched into biological models mimicking the brain more closely. With the advent of quantum computing, we may experience orders of magnitude faster computing and some have even conjectured this is the key to a conscious machine, though I remain skeptical. Regardless of what we call it, the power of it is fully evident and affecting our daily lives already. The potential is both awesome and frightening.

If I use the term *wealth* without a qualifier such as *mental* or *spiritual*, the reader can assume I am referring to traditional material wealth accrual. The word itself, wealth, is problematic and carries with it a lot of baggage but it's short and to the point. I use it to mean in most connotations: abundance, plenitude, fullness and profusion and less so luxury and opulence. This is similar to the usage in the phrase "a *wealth* of knowledge." Wealth also has a convenient matching adjective, wealthy, that other synonyms are lacking. The reader is free to substitute the word of their choice but please try to look beyond the word to the conceptual meaning. Wealth can certainly have a negative connotation for some but for argument and consistency, I am *defining* it as positive and desirable when applied to the right things and in the right way. I will use wealth to indicate a positive form of accrual of certain assets, be they physical, mental or spiritual.

Below, I introduce some unbelievable and possibly disturbing concepts to some. As a philosopher, I will also ask many unanswered questions. I leave it to the reader to ponder these things and to imagine what sort of world is possible, what sort of world we want and where all this is going.

The Current World

Before making a case about the trends and problems in society and what to do about them, of which there are many, it would be valuable to first take stock of present day conditions. No one wants to hear about a solution awaiting a problem to solve. In simplest of terms, society is faced with three major problems:

> **Ecological Degradation:** Pollution, ecosystem collapse, climate change, carcinogens and other toxins and mass extinction

> **Diminishing Resources:** Overfishing, deforestation, lowering oil and coal reserves, lack of food and water in many places, overmining

> **Wealth Disparity:** The dwindling middle class, large pockets of poverty throughout the world, refugees and over-migration, unequal access to good healthcare.

Even if the "war on poverty" succeeded and we could solve problem number 3, if it were done at the expense of 1 and 2, it would have to be considered *unsustainable*.

It is Human Nature, and possibly Animal Nature, to care most about oneself and one's immediate surroundings. However, in a closed system, and the Earth is very nearly a closed system, there is a danger in only caring about what goes on in your neck of the woods, especially if the other neck of the woods is on fire. For whatever one may think about one's own town, state or nation, the Earth has no concept of these man-made constructs. What happens elsewhere can eventually have a huge impact on you or your children or their children so it is foolish to turn a blind eye just because your weather is nice today or your area hasn't experienced a Natural Disaster *yet*. In fact, you may even be a perceived beneficiary of what is a problem elsewhere. For example, some northern locales may experience more temperate living conditions while southern ones become unbearable or even unlivable. If it truly is Human Nature not to care about such things so long as *you* are fine then there may be no hope. I don't believe this to be the case.

Besides the major problems, there are also other large, if not self-inflicted problems, that will be addressed below including:

Overworking: Being forced by society to spend one's days, and often nights, working at a job one does not particularly enjoy and also to be taught that this is the way it has to be.

Overpopulation: Continued steady growth of the world's population has the closed system of the Earth straining to accommodate and is a large contributor to the main problems mentioned above.

Fatigue: Chronic fatigue of several sorts has become commonplace because society does not reward rest but only work.

Mental Problems: Depression, anxiety, insomnia and general unease have been steadily increasing across the globe, especially among the youth.

On top of all this comes the ever-increasing use of AI-driven and plain automation that is already having a significant impact on many careers and vocations including:

Factory workers and assemblers (This led the way years ago)
Warehouse and shipping
Operators, tech-support and receptionists (Smart answering and support systems)
Certain types of musicians and composers (drum machines and AI composers)
Certain agricultural jobs

These initial losses are soon to be joined by a much wider field including but not limited to:

All transportation and delivery-related jobs
Garbage collection and sorting
Legal and accounting services
Home care and cleaning services
Landscaping
Various medical related services
Certain programmers
All manner of agricultural jobs

In this phase, these automations provide greater profits for the company owners via higher production at lower costs but as time goes by, if nothing is done to mitigate, there will be an inflection point where vast swaths of underemployed "consumers" will no longer be able to afford the products and services offered and thus diminishing returns on the automation.

Given these stark realities we face, I have set out to illuminate a highly optimistic and practical path, as outrageous as it seems, that turns automation into our salvation, coupled with sweeping, friendly, democratic social changes and a reprogramming of how we think about our lives, our time, our jobs and our purpose. The end result puts technology in its proper place as a as an extension of our minds and body, in harmony with Nature.

Read what follows carefully, and in its entirety, because each part is connected to the proper understanding of the intent of this treatise: To discover our true Human Nature, our purpose, and how everything we need to be healthy, happy and beyond prosperous is within our reach as a species.

NOTE: See Appendix B in which there are two surveys to assess the psychological aspect of both not mitigating and also highly mitigating these rather dire circumstances.

Chapter 1: The Forms of Wealth

To accrue or to gather certain things speaks nothing of the things themselves. One can gather a pile of leaves, a pile of gold coins, a pile of cigarette butts, but only one of these is thought of as treasure. In general, these gathered items can be called *assets*, their value to be determined. There are Three **Grand Domains of Accrual,** each with subdomains:

Physical: Tangible things

> Material: Matter, energy, goods and things

> Biological: Food, air, water, other needs

Experiential: Learned things*

> Disciplinary: Learning through practice and teaching

> Circumstantial: Learning through experience

Ephemeral: Intangible things

> Spiritual: Karma, mitzvah, love

> Symbolic: Money, digital

> Unknown: The mysterious

*We can't quite be said to accrue that which we are born with but we do start with some innate knowledge. For example, how to use a nipple or to cry when we are hungry. Other animals are born with even more natural skills such as how to walk.

One can accrue assets in each of these domains and subdomains, by luck, inheritance or activity and these assets have quantitative properties as well as qualitative such as:

> The perceived amount or quantity as: wealth, nominal, poverty, debt

> The perceived value or worth as: treasure, nominal, low, garbage

To accrue many assets does not necessarily make one wealthy, since it just as well could make one eccentric or even mad to accrue too much of certain worthless or toxic things. Notice the careful use of "perceived" because so often there is subjectivity involved when it comes to determining the amounts and values of certain assets. "One man's garbage is another man's treasure," is often recited to memorialize the relativity of perceived value.

Garbage and waste are a natural byproduct of any chaotic system of which Life on Earth certainly qualifies. However, these are by no means limited to the physical domain and do accrue in the biological, mental and spiritual domains as well and just as profusely. Cells build up garbage or gunk that eventually kills them. We hear phrases such as "Garbage in, garbage out," or "Who put that garbage in your mind?" and the word garbage is often used to denigrate thoughts and ideas. *One important goal of society is to minimize garbage and waste in all domains.*

For each type of accrual, there is also a corresponding form of *decrease* or *disposal*. Therefore one is not doomed to accumulate garbage (physical or mental) or unneeded assets with no recourse. This becomes more important to society as it grows and produces more waste and it is generally crucial to any personal quest for well-being also. However, many accruals are irreversible (without an actual time machine). Also, decrease or disposal of accrued assets can be involuntary as a result of circumstances, destruction, theft, appropriation, ignorance, foolishness, etc.

The Five Wealths

Wealth is a result of accrual. Here, wealth is defined as *the abundant accrual of high-value assets (assets belonging to the type of wealth)*. Below will be described five distinct forms of human wealth though they are all governed by an intangible overlord we can refer to as Fate or Fortune (to lesser or greater degrees) these forms are:

Physical Wealth: The possession/inheritance of good and clean physical circumstances, free from regular danger, toxins and accidents.

Genetic Wealth: The possession/inheritance of good genes which give one various advantages in society such as good looks, height, smarts or longevity and good health or a combination thereof. This can also be thought of as Biological Wealth but I leave that for a larger purview of the Biological Domain.

Mental Wealth: The possession of a healthy mental state, good training and education and an appreciation of life.

Spiritual Wealth: The possession of a feeling of connectedness, higher purpose and a feeling of a realm beyond our senses

Material Wealth: The possession of money and material things that are said to have value such as gold, property and art.

For a given wealth type, to possess a high amount is to be *wealthy* and to possess little of it is to be *poor* or *impoverished*. One can also possess a nominal amount of wealth, neither rich nor poor. A person can possess any combination of these forms and many of these are completely interdependent. Physical Wealth is listed first since it is the prerequisite for all other wealth types, except for Spiritual. Even if one is born with great genetics into a dire landscape where water and food are scarce or polluted or war is all around, one's odds are greatly reduced for a long and prosperous life. Then, Genetic Wealth because if you are born with certain genetic traits, you may suffer in your ability to achieve abundance in other areas. For example, it has been found that men of average height or less don't tend to get promoted to higher positions as often as those with above average height. It has also been found that women are regularly discriminated against based on their genetics, which is ironic since men are actually the ones who are more genetically mutated since we all start as female[1]. Mental Wealth can overcome most other deficits because to be mentally wealthy is to be mostly happy and content in a creative, interesting life. Spiritual Wealth can free you of most material needs for your well being. Picture a yogi meditating in a cave with no possessions with a big smile on his/her face. Spiritual wealth can overcome most other deficits and in this sense, it is the highest form of wealth. Finally, the lowest form of wealth, Material Wealth is neither bad nor evil, but it is not as valuable as the other forms in terms of actual well being in the long run. Most people possess some form of material wealth. Material Wealth without other forms of wealth inevitably leads to a meaningless, unhappy existence.

Each wealth type can be said to define its own *values*, i.e. the things by which it is ascribed value to and by how much. Those with high value are said to be *valuable*. Values, from one wealth type to another, are generally not transferable though they can greatly impact potential for other types of wealth. As Jesus was quoted "A rich man can no more pass into the Kingdom of Heaven than a camel through the eye of a needle." In other words, material wealth has no value in the spiritual realm (according to Christianity). However, a genetically wealthy person may find the path to fame and fortune much easier than without. One type of wealth can be exchanged to gain access to other forms of wealth, for example, paying tuition (material) to get an education (mental). Also, one form of wealth can foster conditions to access and accrue other forms.

For each type of wealth there is also a corresponding *poverty*, or lack of wealth. Placed on a curve, one would find that each wealth also has an average level where a person is neither rich nor poor in the particular wealth. We might call the absolute dearth of a given wealth type the lowest possible amount of that sort of wealth, Zero Wealth. However, there are many times where we can go further and speak of *Negative Wealth*, or *debt*. All physical debts are temporal in nature and can only be paid back up until the point at which one's Physical Wealth becomes zero, also known as Physical Death. However, it is believed by many that one might incur Spiritual Debts as well. The timeframe for payback of spiritual debts can be far longer than those for physical ones, relatively speaking, although the concept of eternal damnation seems to be preposterous overkill for Earthly transgressions, if one takes Eternity to mean *infinity years*.

When we use the phrase "the war on poverty," we are mostly speaking of material and physical wealth but enlightened folks broaden this to be a war on mental, genetic and spiritual poverty as well since they are all tied together. All of these are in fact being worked on by many good people. Educators spend their time trying to enrich students with Mental Wealth. In general, we can agree that many types of poverty are undesirable and have negative relative consequences.

One supposes it is possible to be wealthy in all the wealth types simultaneously, to a degree. A highly emotionally balanced and knowledgeable scholar could soar to a degree of being a "mental billionaire" but this might not allow time to pursue other things such as physical conditioning or material wealth. We don't see a lot of billionaire professors, though mentally speaking, they are quite wealthy. Conversely, many a financially wealthy person is lacking in education, morals or mental well-being. There are those rare gems who have struck it rich in all categories.

---

[1] https://www.ncbi.nlm.nih.gov/pubmed/4470128

Mental wealth is possibly a subgenre of physical wealth because if one suffers brain damage it becomes much harder to accrue some parts of mental wealth. It has been separated out to emphasize its importance in our temporary lives and as a means to happiness and well-being.

In the end, accrual of any wealth requires the passage of time, and for us mortals that is in *very* limited supply, on average 75-80 years. Even if life expectancy soars, the allotted time before an accident or eventual demise will remain *very* finite.

The parts that make up a particular wealth, that which one accrues, can be referred to as that wealth's **assets**.

Each asset has a **cost** of acquisition. The cost generally boils down to another asset that is traded, most profoundly, *time*, because time, the Primary Cosmic Resource (see below), can't generally be traded for more time, regardless of other wealth one might possess.

Ancillary Wealths

There are any number of subtypes of wealth, both arbitrary and also by importance to one's own well-being. By calling it a subtype, it is not necessarily diminished in importance because there is a bigger category that includes it, such as Mental Wealth. Some of these subtypes could in fact be as important as the parent categories they belong to because lacking such wealth could lead to misery. Here is a partial list:

Biological Wealth: That one was born human and not as a shrimp or worm for example (though they too have wealth and poverty in their domains)

Social Wealth: Friends and fame and ability to socialize and the quality of the society in which one lives*

Moral Wealth: A high set of ethical standards recognized by society

Political Wealth: Cronies, connections, incumbency, oratorical skills

Agricultural Wealth: Crops and livestock to live on and share

Athletic Wealth: Natural gifts of vision, peripheral vision, reflexes, coordination, strength, speed, etc.

Musical Wealth: Composing or improvising skills, instrumental or vocal skills, sheet music, recordings

Cyber or Digital Wealth: Security, bandwidth, not having been hacked, excellent web presence, lack of searchable negatives, good passwords

Trade Wealth: Particular, hard-earned skills in a given trade such as Magic or Carpentry

Criminal Wealth: Wealth that is stolen or ill-gotten, a criminal mind

Generally, these are subgenres of the other Primary Wealth types, often in interdependent combination.

*Social Wealth is so important that it nearly qualifies as a Primary Wealth type but I believe it to be reliant on too many of the other primary types to be easily separated out.

Societal Wealth

Like the individual, societies can also aggregate analogous wealth types by increasing the average wealth of its constituents. Likewise, any societal grouping or unit such as family, club, neighborhood, town, state, nation, etc. could also be said to have a level of each wealth type and some more of one than another. Take a group like Mensa where a higher IQ is required for membership. Overall, we might expect this group to have higher than average mental and genetic wealth but we'd need to know a lot more to say for sure. There could just as well be a lower degree of happiness or a higher degree of mental illness that corresponds to this group. In general, measuring societal wealth is difficult and falls into the realm of statistics, demographics and anthropology.

We currently do employ numerous measures of societal wealth such as the GDP or Happiness Index but the complexities of true wealth are not so simple. A happy society that is about to be subsumed by rising oceans might not know how low its physical wealth is or be able to do anything about it so there could even be a delusional component to it.

Ideally, the Earth taken as a whole could get to a point where we have maximized all wealth types across all borders.

The Four Importances of Wealth

With each type of wealth and assets there are four kinds of importance associated with them:

Internal importance: The importance to the one possessing the wealth or asset.

External importance: The importance that others or society at large place on a type of wealth or asset.

Historical importance: The importance that the future will place on wealth or assets that are no longer possessed.

Cosmic importance: The importance of wealth relative to other possible inhabitants, Divine or otherwise, of the Universe or perhaps the Cosmos itself, or even absolute importance, if it exists.

The *impact* of one's wealth will be higher the further down this list one goes and also the less probable one's accrued wealth would be considered to have an impact, as important as it might be to the possessor. This would also be dependent on the type of wealth or asset one is/was in possession of. Someone who displayed great material wealth and was treated deferentially at every turn because others placed import on this display of wealth could easily be forgotten the moment they died if they had no other wealth types or assets. This is typical of someone with no historical importance. A narcissist may place great import on his own thoughts and deeds that aren't shared by others who remain unimpressed. A humble servant may never appear to have any material importance yet be extremely important to others they have helped or perhaps on a spiritual level beyond the mundane.

The Simple Wealth: Material Wealth

Material wealth, as defined (an abundance of valuable possessions or money), is an illusion. So much of life is determined by the pursuit of wealth or dealing with the effects of others pursuing it. This type of wealth has such a grip on our collective conscience that it *is* what most people refer to as Wealth, as though it were the most important and only wealth that existed.

Upon closer inspection, wealth is a mental construct of one species of animal, *homo sapiens*. What started in a pursuit of basic needs—food, water and shelter—has led us to an overabundance of bad food, foul water and a warming planet instead of merely a warm home. Material wealth has *no intrinsic value* to life on planet Earth. It serves little physical purpose. Ironically, as will be shown below, all material wealth was given to us *free of charge* by the Cosmos and has no actual finite monetary value other than the imagined finite value we give it. We may as well say it has infinite value because no amount of money could buy it if it didn't already exist. What's the cost of an atom? An electron? A photon? What's the cost per minute of gravity or electromagnetism?

We got the Sun for free. All the gold, diamonds, oil and raw resources were also deposited by the Cosmos long ago, free of charge. Every raw material on Earth is free of charge from the Cosmos (See Cosmic Resources below). There is actually potentially a very high price to pay for using (or not using) these free materials foolishly. The price is much higher than money can buy.

It's not that Material Wealth has no practical value, it's that it has no absolute monetary value. When goods are produced automatically or given to us, the cost is nothing. More succinctly, the value of material wealth is relative. If everybody were poor, then modest wealth appears greater than if everybody were wealthy in which case it appears lacking. If everything is free, then everybody is wealthy.

Economists will tell us that it is by adding our labor to raw materials that they gain value but even that is an illusion easily proven with a simple thought experiment. We could now build a set of robots, that could build more robots themselves and using Artificial Intelligence they could also write the software controls and improve the chips and parts they were made out of. These self-making robots are called *Auxons*[2]. Auxons[3] could perform mining, smelting, transport and assembly. Auxons could therefore fully subsume our labor role (the word robot comes from the Czech word for work). Auxons could construct a car, drill for oil, refine the oil, deliver the oil and pump the gas with *no human labor* involved (or lithium and make the batteries for electric cars). In other words, they could take the *free* raw materials provided by the Cosmos, move them around, transform them and deliver them to us using only free energy provided by the Sun or nuclear

---

[2] **Robots to make robots at ABB's new $150 million factory in China**

https://www.reuters.com/article/us-abb-robots-idUSKCN1N109X

[3] https://en.wikipedia.org/wiki/Self-replicating_machine#Lackner-Wendt_Auxon_replicators

energy, at no cost to us*, involving no human labor. Therefor *labor itself has no intrinsic absolute value* since the same thing can be achieved for free. These freely created products are referred to here as Cosmic Products, where intelligence has acted upon and transformed Cosmic Resources into useful or desirable things.

*This "free" assumes that the entire chain of energy production, the creation of efficient solar cells, the power plants and transport of materials to those plants have been subsumed by auxons. The actual Energy, one of the Primary Cosmic resources comes with the Universe.

Let's assume the initial cost to get the auxonic system going was 100 billion dollars where humans were involved in the initial engineering and materials. But then the auxons at some point would take over all roles and so that initial cost could be amortized over centuries, eventually approaching zero. Labor is shown in this experiment to have no intrinsic value since it is made free and so we may upon further examination find that even human labor has no intrinsic value other than an arbitrary, imaginary one we ascribe so the initial cost is also somewhat imaginary. *Labor is only as valuable as we say it is or our imaginations make it.*

$$R + L + I = C \Rightarrow 0 + 0 + I = \text{Imagined (Cognitive) Cost and Value}$$

$$R = \text{cost of Resource}; \; L = \text{cost of Labor}; \; I = \text{Imagined value}; \; C = \text{total Cost}$$

Now to a Capitalist, this seems like a nightmare—everything for free, nothing to charge for and no profit to be made. But this is only a *homo sapiens* issue. Any other species is already quite familiar with this. What does a Robin care about? Where it can find the next worm or twig for its nest or how good the Sun feels or how it will find a mate. How about your pet cat? Never will work a day in its life yet will enjoy a great life of feeding, petting and hunting in the yard for the robin. In fact, each other species has reached an apex of sustenance living, where material wealth is still food, water and warmth. Actually physical wealth *is* material wealth in this case. Yes, because of our rich minds, we need more to be happy. We need love, entertainment, dialog and beautiful things. But the things we need are not material wealth, they are spiritual and mental wealth. Without the mental wealth to appreciate entertainment or beauty, we have next to nothing.

However, even the most successful capitalist would have to admit, if they looked around their estate and saw all manner of material wealth and it happened to all be delivered to them, free of charge, and their neighbor likewise was so provisioned, that it would be preposterous to insist that it *must* cost something instead of being free. Everybody likes a good deal and free is hard to beat when it comes to luxury. If they were to then still insist the true nightmare is that they have no advantage, materially over another, then they would admit to a type of *sociopathy* or desire for another to suffer unnecessarily for the sake of *feeling* superior.

As the saying goes, *you can't take it with you when you go*. And on front end of life, you enter the world with nothing but your birthday suit. The wealthiest king or queen of yore has zero dollars today, no gold and not even a single photon to his/her name at this point and was also born naked. Perhaps said best in Genesis 3:19, "In the sweat of thy face shalt thou eat bread, till thou return unto the ground; for out of it wast thou taken: for dust thou art, and unto dust shalt thou return."

This is perhaps the ultimate expression of the meaninglessness of material wealth, its ephemeral and temporary nature. The Cosmos provides us all with life, all materials need to sustain it and then takes all material away from us at the end. So whatever one thinks one gathered for oneself, that one "possessed," never actually *belonged* to the possessor.

On Possession of Things

Possession of external things is also an illusion, or more exactly, a delusion. There is no objective thing that *proves* ownership in the sense of a mathematical proof. Who owns the Sun or the Earth or the Moon? Who owns the Air you breathe? It would be preposterous to claim ownership of parts of the Cosmos, yet we do it all the time. This is *my* land, *my* house and *my* car. No, you *live* on that land, in that house and drive that car but you do not own them as we all can see when you die, disproving your claim, because there is no *you* to own them at that point. You never did, but *you did believe you did*. Possession can always be traced back to an imaginary, delusional claim.

When settlers arrived in the New World, they claimed land as theirs (in the name of another imaginary land far away) and then used force to defend against any other claimants of said land or to evict them. But that land evolved over eons before them, with no need for them and independent of them and their forebears. They drew an imaginary line around the land and killed trespassers of this imaginary line and often expanded the boundaries with force. Then other people made agreements with them that they could own that land and they could own their land and so Towns, Counties, States and Nations were eventually formed. A Nation is merely a larger imaginary border with compacts between the inhabitants regarding governance and property.

We no more own land than a bird owns a tree they landed on. From space, there are no lines. On a raw biological level, temporary possession often requires killing something or someone or otherwise dissuading competitors from assuming possession. Most possession is temporary at best. Even something as basic as food is possessed only temporarily and though consumed, moves quickly on in the circle of life. Of course, we have civilized ways of procurement too, such as the exchange of tokens or money but when one traces back to the roots of the value chain, something was forcibly taken from another at some point to prop it up. That is our violent inheritance but we rarely consider this as we take "possession" of things.

Not all humans share the same beliefs regarding possession. In some cultures, the idea of land ownership is preposterous, in others it's a God-given right. Therefore, it is not an absolute concept but a social construct. Even in a modern nation, such as the Soviet Union (now defunct) or China, communist governments, land was/is collectively owned, not by individuals.

The Assets of Material Wealth

A person with material wealth has accrued (earned, inherited or purchased) assets such as:

Money and savings
Stocks and bonds
Art
Real estate (land and buildings)

Vehicles (cars, boats, planes)
Gems and jewelry
Home appliances and furnishing
All manner of services
Business assets
Plentiful, high-quality food
Insurance
Books
Sporting goods
Collections
Gadgets
Memberships
Political leverage
Fame

Material Wealth is generally not as important as we may imagine it to be, historically or cosmically. We remember very little of this or that random wealthy person, who may or may not even have existed, depending on the accuracy of records kept. It's not that interesting. What they did with their wealth may be another thing altogether but if they were only wealthy and lived a mundane, material life for themselves it amounts to nothing in the eyes of future generations. This is not to say that the effects of material wealth or those with it are not very real or that they are imagined—quite the opposite! This form of wealth is said to be simple because it is easiest replaced by automation and thus has no intrinsic value outside what the Cosmos provides for free.

Material Poverty

Unfortunately, in the present world, a lack of material wealth is synonymous with *poverty*. Across the world, those that are without food, without decent housing or access to education and medical care are those without money or material assets to claim. Therefor they can not participate in the exchange for goods, often suffering greatly. Whatsmore, often they have been stripped of the security of earlier generations' tribal and communal life living off the free land and forced to live in a game with different rules, operated by "owners" of things.

Many of the World's most intractable and life-threatening problems can be traced to the pursuit of material wealth, resources and false ownership. For example, many wars and Climate Change are caused by such pursuits and disagreements arising from the improper use of resources and the rights to access to them. Over the centuries, the spoils of war, the plunderings, are in the form of taking resources, land and material wealth away from those who had claimed prior possession or not believed in possession. In this way our violent inheritance is very much our violent present and is still quite primitive.

In the Cosmic Age (see below), Material Wealth becomes mostly Physical Wealth because its assets are either no longer relevant or are simply a baseline component of life no longer purchased using a monetary system but widely available on demand, or gifted to us. Material poverty will be no more possible than the Sun not coming up in the morning and the causes of war will also wane with these things, not unlike the way the violent and molten, primal Earth eventually cooled down.

The Foundational Wealth: Physical Wealth

Many might insist that Physical Wealth is the *only* type of wealth, and that all others derive from the world of physics and matter and to some extent, they would be right. So it is perfectly reasonable to call the other types subtypes of physical wealth. However, there are sufficient reasons to separate other types for logical and even metaphysical reasons, leading to the qualification of Physical Wealth as the *Foundational Wealth*.

Many aspects of Physical Wealth are common to many people—the Universe, the state of the Environment, Atmosphere and Water. In many cases, the effects of degradation in these areas impacts certain places disproportionately, for example, in an island culture that is getting drowned by rising sea levels while those on higher ground are not impacted. This also can be dependent of the Mental Wealth of those in power, who make the laws and policies and whether or not they understand the implications of those policies.

The Assets of Physical Wealth

Physical Wealth is the Foundational Wealth and requires the possession of good Fortune with respect to the world around us including these assets:

A hospitable planet that supports life
Life force that can work through common matter
A working brain and heart
Access to Good sleep and rest
Plentiful clean air and water
Safe neighborhood zones
Good roads and infrastructure
Good schooling
Good medical care
A comfortable climate
Quiet and peace
Good, healthy food
Accident-free living
A safe home
A mate and progeny
Sex and pleasure*

*Sex and Pleasure are shared assets between physical, mental and even spiritual domains and are essential for the enjoyment of life and well-being including in their higher forms of ecstasy and bliss. A life without pleasure is pure suffering. A life without suffering is not yet complete.

So much of physical wealth is out of our personal control and depends on the circumstances of one's birthplace, one's parents and the actions of other Global Citizens. One gets little choice about birthplace, or the decisions of one parents to move from one place to another. One also has little choice in matters of displacement by natural disasters or war. We get little say about what happens far away such as a nuclear plant blowing up and spreading radiation around the globe. We certain get no say when Cosmic-level cataclysms such as supernovae come our way.

We live in a world where Material Assets are readily exchanged for Physical Assets which is to say one pays for things that one needs or to live where one lives. Such is the system we have made for ourselves, soon to be obviated.

The understanding of Physical Wealth can change over time as new things are discovered or known things are better understood. For example a home that was once merely well-painted became a hazard once the effects of lead on the brain were known.

Physical Poverty

Physical Poverty has many forms. Some are more important, such as having clean air to breathe. Some are subjective such as seeing cables and wires and unsightly billboards everywhere you look. Some is personal. Some is local. Some is universal. Some is the result of Nature's actions. Some is due to human actions. Some is acute. Some is chronic. Some can be mitigated by material and mental wealth, some cannot.

A Dearth of personal Physical Wealth (zero) results in physical death. No amount of material wealth could buy your way out of a supernova of the Sun, or physical death of any sort. Even if one had one's body frozen for future resuscitation and it succeeded, it only means one didn't actually die. If, on the other hand, one were eaten by a school of piranhas, one has actually physically died. Death in that case begat life as the piranhas were supercharged for the rest of the day and you became fertilizer for new life! Death often does have such repercussions, so in a way, death is a form of Energy Transformation as when light is absorbed into a leaf and the light appears to have died a green death from the outside but thrives on the inside of the plant.

The Lucky Wealth: Genetic Wealth

We all know those lucky gifted or beautiful people who were born with it. They are often said to have good genes. When you are blessed with good genetics, which goes far beyond the superficial aspects of physical beauty into the strength of your immune system, your organs and muscles and so much more, you are very lucky, for you possess *Genetic Wealth*. However, even the most handsome face or body can be marred by scars or befell by accidents and so to be lucky in this regard requires possession of plenty of *Physical Wealth*.

Genetic Wealth is in many ways a subset of Physical Wealth because it relies on certain molecules arranged in such and such a way within your DNA. Lack one bit here or there and you go from healthy to compromised very easily. Most of this is inherited from our parents and their ancestors but there are many ways DNA mutations can take place independent of inheritance.

The Assets of Genetic Wealth

Genetic Wealth requires the possession genetics that can give the possessor assets such as:

High intelligence
Fast reflexes
A good immune system
Well formed organs and muscles
A symmetrical, pleasing face, i.e. good looks
Good hair and skin
Average or above average height
Freedom from congenital defects
Longevity
Natural talent

Since both Physical and Genetic Wealth are governed by physics and biochemistry, it is plausible that today's genetic wealth will be tomorrow's poverty. In other words, we are close to mastering the correction of genetic defects and moreover, the deliberate enhancement of the Human Genome. Designer babies may not have many defects to speak of in the future. And if nanobots learn how to repair bodies or we can master regeneration, even physical trauma may be repaired to a point where we all have much greater physical wealth as a baseline. If one commits suicide in front of a train, it's probably because one's Mental and/or Spiritual Wealth had ebbed too low to protect one.

Astrophysicist and thinker, Stephen Hawking, wrote that he believed we would create a race of superhumans, essentially creating our own obsolescence and likely extinction. This is a distinct possibility now that gene editing has become routine. In this there is a threat that current day material wealth could determine who gets to create these beings for the ultimate purpose of creating a permanent underclass of genetically inferior people. Also, the laws of unintended consequences come into play and such playing of God could lead to a disaster for all of humanity.

If one thinks this is unlikely then run through a hypothetical visit to a future baby consultant where one is asked, "Would you prefer your baby to have above average or below average intelligence? Would you like your child to be short or tall? Do you want your male to go bald or keep his hair? What color eyes and hair do you prefer your child to have?" As one can see, to alter these factors changes the natural course of genetic evolution and it's hard to imagine parents opting for a short child with below average intelligence or any number of a la carte options.

One of the dangers of twiddling around with genes is a resultant lack of diversity. We might see the same "model" of people appearing amidst us with their perfect faces and physiques, thinking and speaking the exact same way as others. One of the greatest Cosmic Gifts is DNA and the way two genomes can merge to create a unique individual from two different legacies of genetics. Sure, we should work to eliminate diseases and certain defects that cause suffering but let's never make ourselves into a colony of clones. A true genetic fortune lies in diversity.

It is our genetic wealth that gives us our potential as individuals and species, but it is our Mental

Wealth that actualizes that potential. Thus did the same exact species fail to develop a printing press, a motor, a rocket and a computer for hundreds of thousands of years, having not acquired sufficient mental wealth to do so. If these were "genetically known" things like a coral knows how to make a fancy shell house for itself, they would have come sooner.

Genetic Poverty

Having defective genes can lead to strife for individuals and entire populations as well and manifests in a large number of ways as complex as the organism itself. Some is inherited, some results from poor nutrition or toxins in the environment. Generally, a species with too much genetic poverty becomes untenable and goes extinct. But also, perfectly health species can go extinct by the actions of another species, most often humankind. Humans regularly snuff out ancient species that were doing perfectly well genetically speaking. Lack of genetic diversity leads to weakness and vulnerability for a species and reduces its chance for survival.

The Superior Wealth: Mental Wealth

Mental Wealth can be thought of as the information we can store in our brains as we live our lives. This requires the capacity to learn and, to a large degree, a healthy body and brain. If we think of the brain and body as our hardware, then mental wealth could be likened to software and data. Software governs *how* we operate and data determines *what* we operate on. In terms of Nature vs. Nurture, this is the Nurture part.

In a lecture at St. John's College, Mr. Robert Neidorf posited that the brain was not only the gray matter up in our skull but the organ of the brain actually permeated our entire nervous system. We are so used to thinking of the brain as the isolated CPU (Central Processing Unit) but Mr. Neidorf made a convincing case for a *distributed brain*. We often speak of "muscle memory" and we know that reflexes take less time to occur than would be required to send the signal to the brain for processing and then send the reply back so it's as though the part of the body has a mind of its own and made the decision for us. In this case the "us" didn't only reside upstairs in the brain but was also distributed through the body which makes some sense. So when we learn certain skills, like playing an instrument, we learn them all around the body in which case "muscle memory" is a real thing.

The amount of information the human brain can store is astounding. Computational neuroscientists have estimated a capacity around 2.5 Petabytes, or 2,500 Terabytes of information. Nevertheless, it is *finite* and eventually can be filled up. Or possibly memory is written over by other memories and knowledge as we age and naturally experience memory loss—hopefully loss at the expense of new gains. The Information Age we are currently in bombards us with much more information than we need and so we may be inadvertently filling up precious storage with garbage—something to consider as you surf around the Internet and your mind "records" your activities. If you can remember it, it must have been recorded! Fortunately, we now have the option to outsource memory and certain types of rote knowledge to devices, cloud services, etc. so we are not doomed to fill ourselves with every spec of knowledge available.

The Assets of Mental Wealth

Mental Wealth requires the accumulation of many assets including (some requiring luck with respect to genetic and physical wealth):

Education (all topics) and language
Knowledge and history
Memes
Appreciation of the arts, music and beauty
The capacity to think critically and philosophize
Emotional stability
Happiness
Mindfulness and awareness
Self-esteem
Mental health in general
Calmness and peace of mind
The ability to simply *be* and feel connected to the Cosmos
Creativity
Imagination
Compassion
Self-discipline
Social skills
Stories and Anecdotes
Courage
Selflessness (humility)
Humor
Spirituality (see below)
Love

This list is far from complete. Even if lacking material wealth in a materialistic world, when one possesses these *mental assets*, one's life will be richer and more enjoyable. There is nothing quite as pathetic as a person of great material wealth who lacks mental wealth and who can never truly be happy, wasting their inestimable days of life. Mental wealth is not given by the Cosmos for free like all the atoms and molecules and photons of the material world are. Mental wealth can only be provided by a series of fortunate events unfolding over time and in a real way—Love. The love of a child for knowledge. The love of parents for their children. The love of neighbors for each other. The love of teachers for their students or profession. Even the love of a society for its people. These are the forces that foster mental wealth starting at day one of life. As the Beatles wisely sung, *Money Can't Buy You Love*. On the other hand, hatred and negativity could lead to mental poverty and unhappiness.

Mental wealth is paramount to answering our question above about what to do with our lives when all material needs are met as the baseline. At the end of the day, we are left with time. Time to do things we love, time with others, time being entertained or entertaining, time alone in meditation, time practicing, time exercising, time enjoying Nature. The key to happiness in a *materially satisfied* world is to enjoy one's time and to help others enjoy their time. Without this, life becomes arduous, a meaningless and literal waste of time.

Mental Wealth has far more true value than Material Wealth. However, Mental Wealth has a fairly large dependency on genetic and physical wealth since it becomes harder to accumulate mental wealth with certain physical limitations. Anthropologists have studied isolated tribes in the Amazon who experience very little, if any depression and are generally quite happy yet live at a simple, subsistence level whereas the industrial world has created entire pharmaceutical and therapeutic industries trying to repair the holes in our broken minds filled with dark thoughts, insomnia, depression and worse. These are forms of mental poverty.

Mental Wealth may very well have, or be, a bridge to inform Spiritual Wealth, but generally speaking, when the brain dies, mental wealth reverts to zero. However, depending on what you did with your mental wealth while alive, much of it can be passed along in the form of memetics, knowledge and teaching so mental wealth is *inheritable*.

Mental Wealth is perhaps the most complex of all the wealth types and comes in the most combinations due to genetics, circumstances, upbringing, society, etc. One could possess for example a high facility in mathematics yet lack in social skills or other interests. Or one might have a musical gift and good social skills but be mentally disturbed to the point of suicide. It is rare to have a good balance of the assets of mental wealth but it should be something one should strive for if possible.

A proper education requires so many years to accrue that it regularly consumes the better part of the first third of our lives. Those that make it to one of the mental peaks generally can see another peak nearby and so this process is truly lifelong and should never stop learning and exploring ideas. The skills one can acquire are so impressive that our greatest achievements as a species fully rely on mental wealth.

Mental Poverty

To be poor in education and experience is to be greatly disadvantaged, ignorant of critical knowledge and incapable of finding solutions to everyday problems. It is to lack appreciation and find little joy in living. Because of the complexity of our minds, it manifests in many ways, some practical and some psychological. To a large extent, society is responsible for causing mental poverty and also enabling mental wealth to accrue. Primal instincts for survival supercede the luxury of developing a higher state of mental acuity and thus society must provide sufficient resources to enable learning and mental health. A society that rids itself of mental poverty is one that accels and evolves to ever greater potentials. One that fosters mental poverty decays and fails.

Mental Wealth has no limits in what it can produce and leads to a quality life worth living.

The Theory of Multiple Intelligences

In his 1983 book *Frames of Mind*, Howard Gardner proposed that human intelligence operated in certain modalities and that gifts of intellect would fall into certain categories including, depending somewhat on genetics:

Musical-rhythmic
Visual-spatial
Verbal-linguistic
Logical-mathematical
Bodily-kinesthetic
Interpersonal
Intrapersonal
Naturalistic

The proposed value of this theory is that if we can identify an individual's predisposition to a certain intelligence, we can foster that through education and maximize the potential of the individual. Inversely, if we squelch access to education in an area of natural talent we may set the individual up for unnecessary failure. This would be important to know as we move into the future as it may help society create happier, more productive citizens.

It has been said that *Ignorance is Bliss* and certainly being ignorant of certain negative things leads to a higher, more peaceful mind. I would say that it is a blessing to be able to clear one's mind and not be overly disturbed by overstimulation and enjoy a pure sense of being which is a rarity these days. In earlier times, it was far easier to have quiet, undisturbed thoughts and to focus deeply on a subject because they had far fewer distractions and didn't have a constant means of entertainment at their fingertips. So please, dear reader, don't confuse quantity of knowledge with quality of knowledge and remember that part of Mental Wealth includes not filling in every mental void with more noise but leaving room for *nothing*.

The measurement of IQ is one of the most overblown and abused metrics and while it does correspond statistically to certain social advantages, it fails to capture the true talents of an individual. As smart as he was, many people could score higher than Albert Einstein yet would never be able to synthesize anything remotely as profound or useful as the Theory of Relativity. Yet he also loved to play violin but couldn't hold a candle to far less intelligent violinists of the time. Pioneers and inventors of many fields possess attributes that can't be easily measured. Some intelligence is laser-focused on a narrow specialty as we see with *savants* and to some degree every creature has such an area of specialty. Cats and dogs are acutely aware of sounds, smells and small movements that we are positively blind and deaf to and on *their* scale we would come up as severely challenged. Dolphins see in sonograms so it's impossible to hide a pregnancy in their honest world. In the end, it's what we do with the intelligence we have that matters.

Mental Poverty manifests itself as dimness, unease, discontent, confusion and general small-mindedness. It can be foisted on us by circumstances, broken homes, poor education and as a result of many failings of society. When an entire society slips into mental poverty, it is very difficult to recover because the chain of knowledge is broken. As Voltaire said, we are always one generation away from Barbarism.

The Meta Wealth: Spiritual Wealth

When it comes to matter of the *spirit*, it is an entirely personal thing. No one can know what you experience due to *qualia*. That some experience *what they call* God or spirits or commune with Nature on a spiritual level is undeniable to *them*. We can all agree that the World provides a certain baseline Mystery for all of us. What happens after we die? What happened before we were born? When did time begin? Is Eternity a thing? Is there a Soul? What is consciousness? Where do we get ethics from? What is Love? Did the Universe get Created or did it evolve or a combination thereof? Each Religion and spiritual practice has its own answers to these questions. Some find peace of mind through meditation, others through prayer and others through Faith. Some want to shout it from the top of a mountain, some want to hold it as a personal belief.

The Assets of Spiritual Wealth

If one does possess spiritual wealth then one possesses things that have no financial value such as:

A sense of well-being and belonging
A connection to the Universe
A higher calling and purpose
A feeling of security about your loved ones, both here and gone
A sense of higher consciousness and beings on a higher plane
A sense that the material world is not as important as it's made to be
A way to deal with mortality
A sense of connection to our ancestors
A center for moral courage
A source of Love and compassion
Enlightenment or Nirvana
Consciousness, sense of being or self
A Soul

While none of us are in a position to say with absolute certainty that such things are real or not, perceived or imagined, we can agree that these can be positive traits that add to Mental Wealth and happiness. An atheist loves their children every bit as as much as a religious zealot. An atheist will at times even pray when a dire circumstance arises and there is nowhere left to turn. You don't have to believe in God to have spiritual wealth.

Spiritual Wealth is the only wealth conceivable that could withstand Death, though there is a concept of Spiritual Death at which point one's *being* would cease to exist. As mentioned, Spiritual Debt or Negative Spiritual Wealth is the basis in many religions for a form of punishment or perhaps requires the debtor to relive life on a lower level or in extreme cases experience Eternal Punishment, which seems a bit too severe but a great scare tactic. Hindus refer to Karma in this regard. Karma is a sort of Spiritual Bank Account, where a positive balance moves one closer to the Godhead and debt requires more or less painful lessons on a lower plane of existence.

Even the most ardent atheist must admit to limits on absolute knowledge and Truth and must admit with regard to consciousness or interdimensional phenomena they don't have the answers. There is ample evidence based on both anecdotes and science that invisible forces have huge effects on us and it's not inconceivable that there is hidden intelligence out there that we don't understand empirically.

Perhaps, by expanding our knowledge of physics and reality and all of its dimensions and hidden forces, we will be able to explain the causes and effects of what we call the Spiritual Realm and the true nature of consciousness. However, even so, it would be found to then exist but play by different rules than we see in the known physical world of today and so understanding it wouldn't necessarily change the fundamental conditions or allow us to subvert or otherwise control it.

For example, if we were to prove that God exists, perhaps a being that evolved over Eternity (an unimaginable "amount" of time), we would not then be in a position to put ourselves above that being.

Extreme Spiritual Wealth could be said to be Enlightenment, Bliss or Nirvana. We imagine this to be the highest state of being, especially those of us who have not achieved it. Many remain skeptical of the existence of these states and actually most of what people claim to be spiritual experiences. Often they are explained scientifically as delusions but they are never fully disproven with scientific or mathematical certainty. People under the influence of certain psychedelic drugs such as psilocybin mushrooms or ayahuasca often have experiences recounted as spiritual in nature and many claim to gain a lifelong benefit, informing perceptions about life, if not only that there are other frames of reference to view the same world and see it completely differently—a valuable lesson.

Spiritual Poverty

Spiritual Poverty is a form of dullness and a lack of meaning in life. Those that have no sense of connection to the glorious majesty of the Cosmos or do not experience true Love or compassion are mere shells of matter bouncing around randomly. Those that lack a sense of mystery can be likened to a sleepwalker, unaware of the incredible dance unfolding before their eyes. This has little to do with religion, which is merely a formalized attempt to normalize and organize spirituality on a social level when in fact it is a personal matter. Society can have a major impact on fostering the natural sense of wonder in children or snuffing it out with overemphasis of practical matters. Philosophical education allows us to ponder life's mysteries and accept that we do not, and cannot know everything and develop a greater appreciation for the splendor of life.

Mindfulness: Where Mental and Spiritual Wealth Meet

To be mindful is to be *present*. It is very easy to be sucked into a pattern of mundane concerns, never taking a break to simply *be* and free your mind of thoughts and so it is easy to fill your mind (or have it filled for you) with anything except for appreciation of the moment you are in. When we learn to take in the moment we start to see the world in a different light. As the Sufi mystic and poet, Rumi, once said, "Stop acting so small. You are the universe in ecstatic motion." By using our minds and our mental wealth, we can develop skills to put us in touch with our higher selves but it requires discipline and practice such as meditation or for some, mindful prayer.

Certain activities can increase mindfulness and should be part of a healthy life:

Communing with Nature
Meditation and yoga
Breathing exercises
Listening carefully
Paying attention
Concentration
Celebration
Listening to music
Appreciating art
Dancing
Prayer

Inheritance: When Wealth Is Passed On

Each type of wealth, except for spiritual, is *inheritable*. There are those that also believe that through reincarnation, one can inherit spiritual wealth by accrual in a prior life. By squandering a type of wealth or spending it all, one can also preclude inheritance for the next generation. Inheritance is a function of Fate because one has no control over what transpires before one's birth. Some wealth is bequeathed such as when it is listed in a Will and others are gained by random circumstances. The following are examples of inheritance applied to the five wealths:

Physical: Being born into a safe country, clean environment or a good home with plentiful food and clean water

Genetic: Inheriting good genes

Mental: Having access to a quality education, books and parents with mental wealth

Spiritual: Good karma or perhaps a high quality "old soul" if such a thing exists

Material: Inheriting the material wealth of one's parents, relatives or friends

Society has been perpetually vexed with certain ill-deserved generational material wealth that is not put to good use other than for the satisfaction of the material desires of lucky children and grandchildren who apathetically play all day with expensive toys, eat at fancy restaurants and jetset around the globe, often eschewing even a proper education. This is perhaps the most worthless form of human in that they consume luxury, have a huge carbon footprint and produce nothing of value. These types are immediately forgotten upon demise. Such Machiavellian efforts have been made to prop up and protect generational wealth that even inbreeding of cousins was common among royals to keep it "in the family."

Fortunately, there are also many philanthropic families who through Trusts and Foundations perpetuate charitable activities and wisely oversee the wealth generated by their ancestor. But society is at constant odds over Estate Taxes and the limitations of inheritance and so shall this problem be solved in the Cosmic Age since money becomes obsolete and material wealth is available on demand. The Trust Fund babies will disappear with the funds or more accurately, everybody will be one. The very meaning of Royalty will become even more anachronistic and absurd than it already is today.

We All Inherit the Earth

One of the great privileges of life is being born onto a beautiful Planet. No amount of money could buy such a perfect thing as the Earth, with its perfect Moon and Sun at just the right distance and its perfect tilt to create the beauty of the seasons and its iron core to create a magnetic shield to protect us from the solar winds. The Earth is perfection incarnate. Everything we are and everything we have we owe to the Earth, Moon and Sun. And they in turn are nothing without the galaxy that provided all of the matter and energy and gravity to keep everything in perfect harmony. We inherit this upon our birth and much more. We get light, sense to perceive that light, mathematics, minds to comprehend that mathematics and more. Below our feet is a molten core of liquid metals including trillions of tons of gold, platinum and every element we all studied in school. But between us and that molten core is a beautiful crust and a very thin layer of life where we breathe fresh air, smell flowers and see the splendor and majesty set before us. Many go through life never truly appreciating this majesty and are stuck on a plane of mundane existence in the world created by mankind. We can't blame them for this because they were not properly raised to appreciate this or the society they grew up in didn't value it so in a way this experience was stolen from them. Every child is born with curiosity and wonder and it is up to society to foster and nurture that child.

In a materialistic world, the Earth represents Owned *Resources*. Resources are to be mined, harvested and used. However, since we didn't purchase these resources, they are actually stolen or borrowed from the Earth. In a sustainable world, they are borrowed and later replenished. In an unsustainable world they are stolen, destroyed and never returned creating an imbalance. The Cosmos operates on very simple principles and everything must be in balance. Over billions of years, the Earth created a perfect harmony between plants, animals, land and sea and air. Humans have upset this balance, largely because we don't understand our role and our responsibilities to upkeep the balance. Typically, such imbalances are handled well by the Earth by extincting the offender. If you try to operate too far out of balance for too long, the systems go haywire as they try to restore the balance. The best example of this is in Climate Change. By burning copious fossil fuels which are essentially ancient sunlight locked up in organic compounds, we are changing the chemical profile of the atmosphere, trapping today's Sun with yesteryear's Sun. This in turn causes air to move around more vigorously, oceans to heat up and results in ever increasing storm sizes, droughts, fires, floods and insect plagues. Such an imbalance can only last so long before the Earth reverts to its primordial, inhospitable self.

The Cosmic Resources: Infinite Value, Zero Cost

Cosmic Resources are common and belong to ALL inhabitants of Earth *equally* because no person or group can rightly lay claim to a domain that existed long before humanity. *Cosmic Resources can not be owned.* These resources can be listed in two main groups:

The Foundational Cosmic Resources:

Time: The Primary Resource, without which no other resource can exist. No amount of money can buy nor destroy time as it operates on a non-material level, independent of all else, requiring nothing but itself to operate.

Space: The Secondary Resource, without which Time would have no effect though Time still would exist without Space. But that is Moot since they co-exist, probably in Reality as co-equals—Space-Time.

Energy: All the energy that exists will continue to exist and be transformed into other forms of energy or matter. Energy imbues Motion to the Cosmos and a Still Cosmos would be devoid of Energy. Energy, if it *can* be said to die, would do so in a Black Hole where it becomes an Eternal prisoner with respect to the outside world. But we know nothing of what happens *inside* the black hole.

Matter: All matter is somewhat illusory in that it is actually "frozen energy" or perhaps vibrational standing waves on an inter-dimensional, nanoscale. Yet it exists and we interact with it, specifically, large groups of atoms and molecules. We don't interact with the particles that compose matter. The closer one looks at matter, the less it seems to exist. For example, atoms are known to be 99.9999999999996% empty space.

Forces: Gravity, electromagnetism, the nuclear forces are forms of energy we can utilize and perceive in action. Without forces, we would have no organization and no matter could interact. Forces are somewhat mysterious as they operate with invisible fields and over theoretically infinite distances.

Quanta: The smallest "Planck" divisions of matter and energy that exhibit "magical" powers such as quantum entanglement that can cause two particles to share states instantaneously over any distance, infinitely surpassing the speed of light.

Harmonics Vibrational relationships that produce octaves and other harmonic intervals that permeate both matter and perceptions. $H2O$ is a perfect example of material octaves and the taste of water is similar to the sound of octaves in music.

Mathematics: The numerical and geometric relationships of each thing to the next and the exact Laws of Reality

Metaphysics: Parallel universes, spiritual realms, extradimensional realms, eternal things, unknowable things

The **Practical Cosmic Resources** (ones we can directly interact with and use):

Sunlight, Wind, Ocean Tides, Molten Magma, Chemical and Nuclear Energy

Elements (eg. Oxygen, carbon, iron, silicon, gold, silver, etc.)

Molecular substances (eg. water, air, diamond, etc.)

Biological resources (eg. Plants, animals, bacteria, oil, etc.)

Ore, geological resources containing elements we desire

Stars, planets, moons, asteroids, etc. (the results of Forces acting on Matter and Energy over Time in Space)

Crystals, a special form of molecules or elements

Undiscovered materials

Most of the World we see and know, is composed of transformed Practical Resources although some of them we enjoy directly, free of charge, such as air when we breathe. We ourselves are such a resource! Practical Resources are transformed in three ways:

Passive: Through natural phenomena such as biological growth or geology (eg. volcanic activity, a tree growing). These naturally transformed resources are still considered Cosmic Resources but of a higher order.

Active: Through animal labor (eg. a sculpture or a bird's nest)

Meta: Through automated "labor" (eg. a mining robot)

The Earth receives daily only a tiny fraction of the Sun's output, most of which flies off at the speed of light in every other direction than the Earth lies. In fact, we only receive approximately one billionth of the Sun's energy radiation. This illustrates the absurd overabundance of the Foundational Energy Resource. Yet, even this belies a much, much larger energy inheritance that is for all practical purposes infinite, for in every single atom is locked up enormous amount of nuclear energy left over from the Big Bang and billions of years of supernovae, neutron stars colliding and who knows what. It's mysterious but very real.

We have set aside certain elements as very special, such as gold and platinum and even carbon, when it's been compressed into the crystalline form of diamonds. In a real sense these substances are *very* special because of the *time* it requires for them to be created. For gold, a star has to collapse into a dense neutron star and then collide with another neutron star. Only then can gold be forged. But when you think about it, every element is just as special, made out of the same miraculous electrons, neutrons and protons that were formed after the Big Bang. Without hydrogen to fuel those stars or gravity to compress them or electromagnetism to coalesce them, gold would not exist.

We even refer to certain of these metals as Precious Metals and others as rare Earth elements due to their relative scarcity in the upper crust of the Lithosphere (crust). However, there is so much gold that settled at the Core of the Earth (along with lead and other such heavy elements) that if brought to the surface could probably coat the Earth in a *very* thick layer of gold making it much less precious and even deadly. So rarity of substance is often equated with value but it's actually lack of access that we value, a sort of anthropocentric supply and demand model. A dog has no use for gold nor a particular attraction to it. Place a steak next to a bar of gold and you'll see.

The undefined or infinite value of Cosmic Resources can be attributed to the Eternity which was available to create them, even if it's a *Relativistic* Eternity. Over sufficient *Time*, something of zero value can become all possible value.

The Cosmic Products: What the Universe Makes For Us

When we have created a sufficient level of automation, to the point of requiring very little, if any, human intervention to manufacture and deliver goods and services, what we are getting are Cosmic Products, those that are made by the organizing principles and materials of the Cosmos itself, a sort of intelligent matter if you will. Organization begets organization. In the exact same way that the Cosmos produced us over eons of evolution, we will likewise produce another System, begat by our own organization and Mental Wealth. In as far as this System is an extension of our own intellects and bodies, it has additional nearly infinite powers hidden in the locked up Mysteries of the Cosmos in the form of mathematics and logic. Software that improves itself, does so without our specific guidance on the finer details once we have pointed it in the right direction. Machines that build improved machines are the physical manifestation of this same principle, i.e. Auxons. Over sufficient time, there is nothing that prevents the Cosmos from Becoming whatever it will be, biologically or otherwise. This force of organization is often referred to Extropy, the opposite of Entropy.

The Programmability of Matter

That matter is programmable is well-understood by any molecular biologist. The study of DNA Code, the pattern or sequence of A,T,C,G along the double helix acts very much as a computer program that is so advanced and sophisticated it can cause matter to organize itself, even into a brain that can think about itself, starting from just two cells! We know it is programmable because we can now edit the sequence to produce different results.

A very similar phenomenon is the foundational generative method of Cosmic Products—we program matter in this case, not to create biological entities, but things to enrich life, protect it and minimize extraneous suffering. A computer is a good example of programmable matter because what is a computer but a collection of well-organized molecules that can be programmed to carry out all sorts of desired objectives? Software shares the sequence trait of DNA. Instead of molecules, it is a sequence of numbers placed into the computer memory and CPU that sends electrons this way and that and causes a cascade of exact actions. So when we create larger systems that can create buildings, roads, transport systems, etc. it is *very similar*, only on a larger material scale. The programmability of matter is a natural phenomenon and Cosmic Products are merely an extension of matter that was already programmed, namely us.

Automata Theory[4] is a well-established formal theory regarding *abstract* machines that relies on

---

[4] https://en.wikipedia.org/wiki/Automata_theory

symbols and language. So one can infer very similar principles where the *alphabet* becomes atoms and *words* become molecules to produce a theory of *concrete* physical machines. Therefore, in a series of finite steps following an algorithm of indeterminate complexity, matter can be placed into possible positions in space and time, energy applied and physical results or output can be achieved. The scale at which this can be enacted ranges from the macroscale (robots) to the microscale (microbots) to the nanoscale (nanobots).

There are few limits in what Programmable Matter can produce for us including:

Delicious, healthy food
All manner of high quality "luxury" goods
Beautiful architecture and living spaces
The finest medical care
Protection against all manner of threats
Exquisite entertainment
Flying machines
Splendid and plentiful gardens, parks and habitats for animals
Scientific instruments
High quality tools and equipment
Fantastic clothing
Space structures
A garbage and pollution-free environment

If you look around you will see many practical things that could be made automatically and then also some that couldn't be, like that drawing your child made hanging on the refrigerator or that photo taken at the perfect moment by an observant photographer. In fact, even if something is made via automation, there may be a human designer behind it or who decided on the design offered by the AI agent before it was materialized. This illustrates the value of Mental Wealth, the ability to creatively direct automation for our needs. But it also shows how automation could be easily misdirected to produce poor designs or even garbage if the director was lacking in aesthetics or good taste or knowledge.

This is perhaps the most troubling concept of this treatise—that so much of what we need could be *magically* provided for no cost! In fact, it's not magical or even far-fetched and it is entirely possible given current technologies and understanding and *the will* of society to do it. If one breaks it down into its logical steps as would an engineer or programmer they might be as follows. For a small proof of concept, a simple, crude model could be created (almost be a high school science team) that could be scaled up:

Set aside a piece of land for our experiment

Create a plan and blueprint for a small community to be created later on the land, after planning. The community will have buildings and pathways and a central park.

Create the plans for a movable large-scale printer capable of building houses and other buildings. They already exist[5].

Have a self-driving truck deliver building materials from a remote source to the staging area. They exist.[6]

Develop an automated system that can move the printer from location to location, similar to the self-driving truck, but far simpler.

Develop an automated system that can unload the delivery truck and transport materials from the staging area to the printer's hopper.

Develop a self-driving bulldozer (autodozer) and grader that are programmed to level a given area 1. They exist.[7]

Move printer into area 1, print foundation and structure while the autodozer grades the next area 2.

Repeat for all structures.

Grade park and develop a similar set of systems to lay sod or plant seeds.

Develop a system than can create all the machines used above.

Develop a small-scale automated energy infrastructure with solar and wind.

Fill in the supply chain back to the source with similar technology.[8]

Expand the system to simple farming.

Deliver foods to the structures.

Expand and evolve the system.

When any part of the supply chain reaches full automation, that part has gone Cosmic. When the entire supply and fabrication chain has gone Cosmic, that is the dawn of the Cosmic Age.

The **Chain of Production** for Cosmic Products can be broken into at least seven major segments including:

Practical Resource Extraction, eg. recycling, mining, forestry, energy harvesting

Transport, Distribution and Handling of Raw Materials

Resource pre-processing, eg. smelting, lumber creation, etc.

Transport, Distribution and Handling of Processed Materials

---

[5] 3-D Printed house—https://www.3dnatives.com/en/3d-printed-house-companies-120220184/

[6] Autonomous Driving—https://www.daimler.com/innovation/autonomous-driving/mercedes-benz-future-truck.html

[7] Autonomous Construction—https://www.autodesk.com/redshift/autonomous-vehicle-technology-in-construction/

[8] Autonomous Trains—https://arstechnica.com/cars/2018/12/mining-company-says-first-autonomous-freight-train-network-is-fully-operational/

Manufacturing, taking pre-processed materials and cutting, assembling, etc.

Transport, Distribution and Handling of Manufactured Goods, i.e. Cosmic Products

Restoration and Recycling, restoring mined and forests areas, moving broken and unused and manufacturing waste materials back into the chain

These processes are often concurrent, employ similar techniques and feedback between the segments acting very much like a living system. In fact, it *must* be approached in a biological manner in full accordance with laws of sustainability and *Systems Thinking* as expounded by the great 20th Century thinker, Buckminster Fuller[9].

If any of this seems too difficult and arduous or technically challenging, remember the purpose: to end the billions of man years of wasted time, pain and suffering we must endure to prop up a failing and unsustainable system. Another way to look at it is the robots are not replacing us but instead *we* are doing *their* work now, *we* are the robots! What is the end of commuting, punching in and out, sitting all day, standing all day, pounding nails all day, dodging traffic all day, endless meetings, the stress of management and labor worth? What is the end of taxation, warfare, poverty, homelessness worth? Surely it's worth a portion of what we now spend on all of these things and more only to perpetuate a system that breeds greed and unhappiness and frankly, disaster.

Automation is a great preserver of time. I used to have a publishing software business called Gluon. We discovered very early on that if there was a repetitive task, the time spent programming an automated solution to that task, that additional effort spent not doing the task, even getting behind on the task, paid off in orders of magnitude later down the line when the program was ready and we let it rip. The ultimate tortoise and the hare. And so did our customers who highly valued our tools to reduce the tedium of modern publishing and these tools are still in use today.

As of the year 2018, the above experiment doesn't even seem technically outrageous. One can imagine what these already existing technologies will be capable of in the very near future, with many more options and more flexibility. Each engineering process has a finite number of steps and the problem can be reduced to an automation algorithm.[10]

One can already see a shadow of Cosmic Products and overabundance in modern society. Americans throw away almost as much food as they eat. Storage units and attics are packed to the ceiling with overflow products we'll never use. City dumps are filled with yesterday's model of lamp or chair or all sorts of things that have been replaced, not out of need but out of abundance and easy access to replacements. Some people even make a living harvesting these products from the waste cycle at no or little cost. We've become so good at making things that in a way *we are the robots* making the free Cosmic Products already.

---

[9] https://www.umsl.edu/~sauterv/analysis/Fall2013Papers/Purcell/bucky.html

[10] The proof of this Automation Conjecture is too large to fit in the margin.

Chapter 2: The Imaginary Nature of Money

We take the value of money for granted. At the dawn of civilization and probably well before that, people traded this thing for that thing or this service for that—a barter system of sorts. At one point in Mesopotamia, records began appearing in the form of trading ledgers and I.O.U's—promissory agreements for future payments and the concept of currency was created. As time passed we started to ascribe more value to certain materials, whether it was salt, fur and then much later precious metals and gems dug up from the ground. At least with salt and fur, you could directly use the material to improve your life.

Then, for reasons of neatness and ease of transaction, we created coins. Coins had no intrinsic value. They couldn't be eaten or drunk. You couldn't stay warm with them and you couldn't build a house with them unless you had an awful lot of them. But they were shiney and fairly hard to make so we called them *valuable*. Why do we prize shininess so much? Perhaps we are no different than moths attracted to a shining light. After shiny coins were invented, you could hand over some coins and someone would then give you something you could actually use. Something useless for something useful. A good trade, one level removed from reality.

Coins became impractical and the accumulation of coins became a burden so we invented paper money that represented a store of "coins" tucked away in a treasury. The promissory note, or legal tinder. Now you could hand someone something even more useless and get back even more useful things. Two levels removed from practical reality.

Fast forward to today where we regularly transfer electronic bits and bytes that absolutely worthless themselves, almost completely imaginary and they in turn represent numbers in a bank account, also imaginary, where the balance goes up and down, yet nothing else in the material world has changed. Just a number. Your bank balance, three levels removed from reality. We have come to accept this ephemeral, electronic money as so valuable that we can buy houses, groceries, college tuition, etc. without so much as seeing a single electron, paper bill, coin or material thing, all on faith in a common, agreed upon delusional value.

Fiat Money, such as the Dollar is an expression of Sovereignty and Faith where a very large "bully," in this case one that can end the World with its nuclear arsenal gets to tell the rest of the World what their money is worth and as long as the world agrees on that value, it seems to tick along. But it remains a story that is told, with no scientific or mathematical proof of value. Hyperinflation that happens to countries from time to time, devalues this imaginary money so quickly that wheelbarrows full of cash are required to buy a loaf of bread, if even. This has happened many times.

Now, we can take it one step further for the Fourth Level away from Reality: Cryptocurrency. This form of money is so nonexistent and imaginary that it doesn't even have the concept of a bank or any other backing institution or treasury involved and the value is made up entirely from thin air by programmers and social networks of investors. Users of cryptocurrency have no idea what they have because it's all locked away in gigantic, ever-increasing in size encrypted *block chains* of theoretically every single transaction ever performed on the currency so each person has a copy of the entire unreadable ledger tucked away in a *digital wallet* that they simply believe in. Basically, cryptocurrency is digital memory. Thus these cryptocurrencies fluctuate wildly from immense imaginary value to worthlessness overnight. Yet there are numerous crypto millionaires and even billionaires out there who have done nothing to earn anything other than buying a crypto low and selling it high. Good work if you can get it. Cryptocoin makers, of which there are thousands, work furiously to tell a story about their new money. It's not money. It's a new way to think of money. It replaces money. Storytelling is the key to cryptocurrency value. A bad story and your bits are worthless. On top of that, blockchains are nothing more than encrypted secret codes and are therefore only as secure as the encryption they are made with. One quantum computer may have the power to decrypt and re-encrypt and completely destroy the value proposition of a given cryptocurrency such as Bitcoin.

At this rate we can anticipate future *thought coins* that don't even have a block chain of numbers on a hard drive or RAM chip somewhere, but only exist in the mind of the owner. Of course, these will be the most valuable coins of all because they will have the least connection to Reality.

If this feels a little like a pyramid scheme where we have built and ever-increasing value out of an ever-dwindling resource that's because it is. Money is the largest pyramid scheme on Earth. And those with lots of this imaginary money have lots of power too. They get to draw lines around more property, buy more things, elect and hire more people to protect themselves and decide who gets a job and who doesn't, who goes to school and who doesn't, who eats and who doesn't, who gets medical treatments and who doesn't, on and on. Even if you examine the origins of this power: inheritance, entrepreneurship, investment you will eventually come to a place where some free resource provided by the Cosmos was exploited by employing free labor (slavery) and some combination of penalty of death, hardship or other physical bullying that was used to exact the arbitrary value that was deposited in some bank account.

Perhaps nothing illustrates the imaginary nature of money than the fascinating story of J.S.G. Boggs, an artist who would draw his own beautiful bills and then convince a restaurant to accept his drawn bill as money, at first not successfully but then was accepted and then grew in value. It wasn't long before Boggs Bills were were worth far more than the money it imitated, selling at times for millions of dollars. Boggs fabricated value out of paper and ink and imagination.

Another interesting way to illustrate the imaginary aspect of monetary wealth is to take a look at a certain "billionaire" who was said to go bankrupt and reported a net loss of a billion dollars on his tax returns (he later became President). No bank would lend him the money and no bank wanted to lose the money he owed so in effect, he owned negative money, or money that was owed to others. Yes, that is worse than having zero money, until it's not. This fellow proceeded to receive a stipend from one of said lending institutions which was later paid off by another more spurious "foreign" lending institution which in all cases are merely moving imaginary ones and zeros out of balances and into others, robbing Peter to pay Paul. Regardless of having less than no money, negative wealth, said "billionaire" was able to go right on with his lavish lifestyle, riding limos, taking private choppers and jets and dining at the finest restaurants. So apparently, if you can make the right people *think* you are rich, you can actually be materially wealthy. You have to have a good story to be wealthy.

Now we have classes of people who use money to buy money that then changes the value of money in a sort of snake eating its own tail myth. And money in one place is not valued the same as money in another place which also shows how money can never be given an absolute value like say a gram or a meter. Ironically, the closest we've ever come to a standard is the Gold Standard, where a measurable mass of gold is deemed to represent X value. However, because the X is still subjective, it fails as a standard.

If we could create a value system based on an absolute, unchanging standard, it would destroy the money economy which is built on imagination and stories. But we can't because we don't actually need money. We can't eat it, breathe it, live in it or stay warm with it.

This is not to say that individuals do not deserve nor did not earn their material wealth, only that if we honestly examine how they got to be that individual, the potential for that wealth inherited from another's labor, another's materials and eventually, the *Cosmic Resources*. Because the Cosmic Resources are of indeterminate or infinite value, any finite division of those resources is also indeterminate and infinite in value—just like math works.

Even when one delves into the mathematical formulae for money, one sees contradictions and subjectivity. For example, playing with the equation for Monetary Exchange[11]:

$$M \cdot V = P \cdot Q$$

where, for a given period,

M is the total nominal amount of money supply in circulation on average in an economy.

V is the velocity of money, that is the average frequency with which a unit of money is spent.

P is the price level.

Q is an index of real expenditures (on newly produced goods and services).

So that $P/M = V/Q$ where the price level divided by the total money in circulation creates a sort of price or value unit, call it *U*. Leaving Q (an imaginary value) fixed, all one needs to do to change the V say from 1 transaction to 2 transactions and U doubles in value. Or if for this period no transactions are recorded, U becomes zero, infinitely less valuable.

It's not that money is not useful or even necessary in our present lives, it's that upon closer inspection, it's not objectively there outside the gigantic pyramid scheme propping it up. Or rather, the pyramid has no base.

All currencies are temporary.

---

[11] https://en.wikipedia.org/wiki/Equation_of_exchange

Another illustration of the imaginary nature of money is to look at how many arbitrary things we have called money and valued as money from culture to culture and time to time:

Animals and food
Salt (from which the word salary is derived)
Rai, large stones from Micronesia
Wampum, strings of quahog shells in North America
Coins of all sorts and materials
Tokens
Tulips
Paper bills
Exonumia: checks, credit cards, IOU's, etc.
PayPal, Apple Pay, Google Wallet and electronic transfers
Cryptocurrency

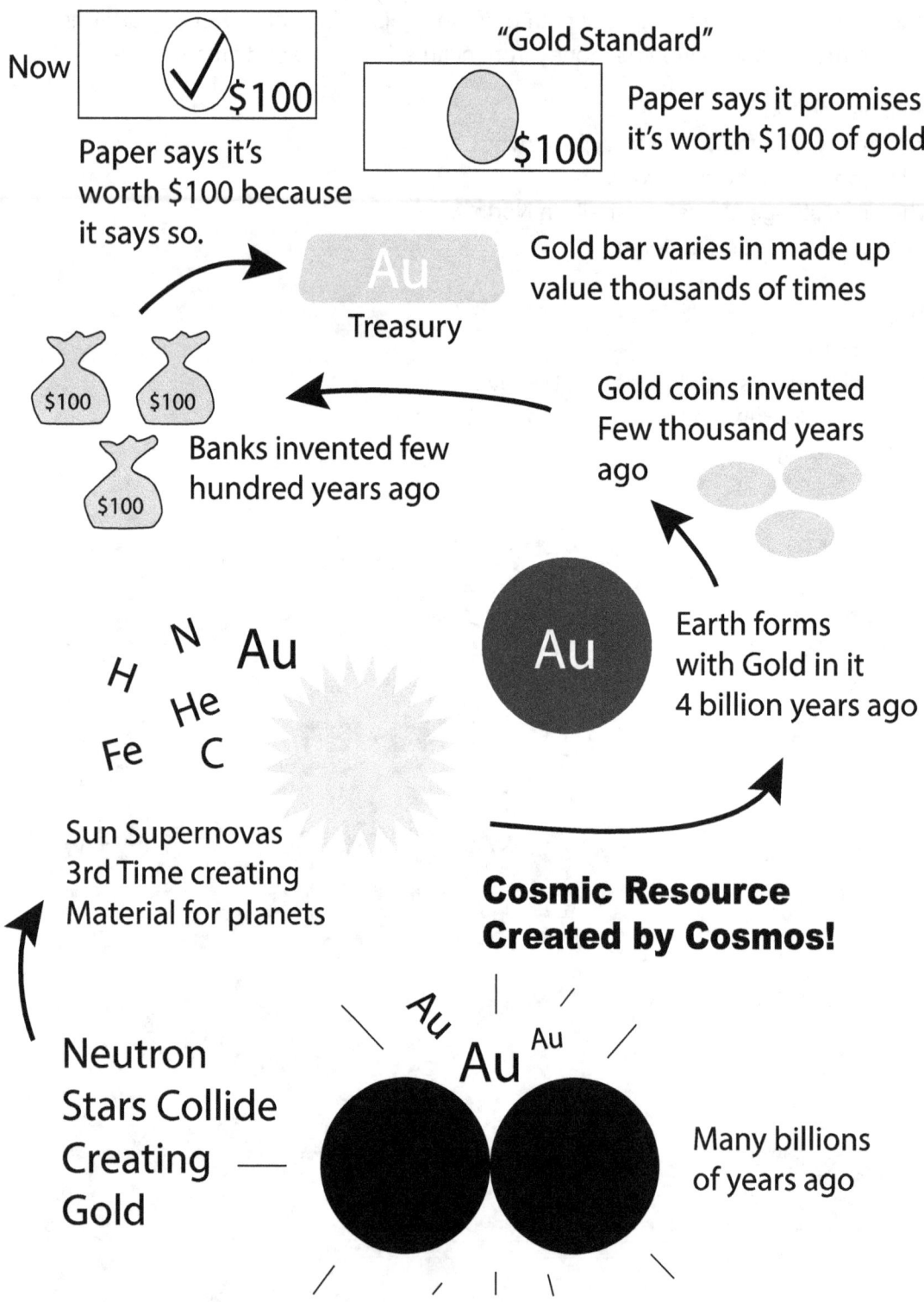

Figure 1. The imaginary nature of arbitrary value assigned to a cosmic resource

Imagination: What Worlds Are Made Of

One can never have too much imagination. There are religions and philosophies that even posit that The World is being imagined in the dream of a higher being or a god if you will. Some have imagined that it is a sort of "computer" simulation (that also simulates people imagining it's a simulation). In either case, it is a Grand Illusion that we must abide by and appreciate as conscious participants.

The Hindus have a word for this, Maya, where the world is a sort of "magic show" and nothing we see is as it actually is. We already have scientifically proven this in many ways. Our senses are limited to a small subset of what is actually there. None of us perceive matter as empty space and it feels very real but upon close inspection, it's nothing like what we see. So illusion and imagination rule our lives.

By saying something is imaginary, it is not intended to demean or lessen its validity, but only to say that the basis of its existence is a particular mental construct that could be imagined in any number of ways and thus is not some sort of absolute Truth, even though many may agree on the construct. It is entirely subjective. This brief regression through the history of money shows an evolution from tangible, practical things to intangible abstract things such as bits and bytes in "the cloud." That is not to say, because they are intangible and abstract they are less real or important but only that they are highly mutable, like the contents of a dream that may shift at any moment.

Imagination plays a huge role in society, perhaps the largest. It permeates our culture on every front from inventions that we use to the books we read and the entertainment we enjoy. Without it, we would still be grunting and groaning and running from cheetahs in the Savanna. Therefor imagination might be the most valuable mental asset we can possess.

One might divide Reality into four cognitive realms:

Tangible and Concrete
Intangible and Imagined
Unknown
Unimaginable

But we need to keep in mind, even though we perceive something to be tangible (touchable), even the act of touching is somewhat imaginary since matter is nearly empty and atoms don't actually touch like we think they do, only their invisible fields repel one another yet we tell ourselves a story that we have touched something. We tend to believe our own stories.

"Beyond imagination" is a phase we often use, sometimes even describing something someone has clearly imagined. We have to admit certain limits in cognition. You have no idea what that electron is actually doing right this moment in your fingernail. Now multiply that times every electron in the Universe and you can quickly see how limited your cognition is. We have developed language around such things, especially in mathematics where we deal with *infinity* and preposterously large and small numbers. We cannot truly grasp the concept of Eternity, a time with no beginning and no end. Many children naturally wrestle with these sorts of thoughts and what happens when you get to the edge of the Universe and want to take one more step or throw a stone but as we get older, many of us give up.

Even in this exercise of trying to trace the true value of money and wealth to its origins we find huge gaps in our understanding and so revert to the status quo of it is what it is and how it must be. To say it is all imaginary is in itself unimaginable to many. One might call that more of a lack of imagination in that case. No matter, we are not meant to contain every thought and every bit of reality in our relatively spec-like minds. We contain placeholders for such things and that allows us to talk about them. Yet there are many things we have no concept of, no placeholders and no language for. These are things that are unknown or beyond our capacity to imagine. But we do know our stories. And they *do* have value.

Banking: Where Imaginary Money Is Managed

One of the most powerful institutions we have created, power over our lives that is, is the Bank. The modern bank is a repository of imaginary dollars on a ledger, often so over-leveraged that the money truly has no presence other than a promise the bank makes to you that they are *good for it*, sort of like your cousin Vinny. You never see it, other than stacks of bills in a teller's drawer or what magically pops out of the ATM after you touch some buttons in the right order. At one point, banks had gold or actual cash on hand that represented their holdings. We all remember *It's a Wonderful Life* when a small bank was ruined when Uncle Billy lost $8,000 (in 1946 dollars).

Today's banks, especially the larger ones, represent their holdings as a portfolio in an ever-expanding pyramid scheme where it's hard to ever see the actual thing they own or lay claim to. Yet they control nearly everything in life because someone told us to believe their story and we did!

Banks are so important to society that many Laws are created to regulate them and how they go about moving imaginary money from this ledger to that one. To violate these laws is a financial crime, punishable by paying large sums of imaginary money or in some cases, time in prison.

However, this is still a legacy system based on the outdated cash model and it is under a lot of pressure to change in the digital age and new financial mechanisms such as PayPal, Google Wallet, iPay, etc. are starting to now abstract the bank a level back, just as we saw with money itself. The ultimate disrupter of the banking sector is cryptocurrency, where the value is locked up in an imaginary self-validating blockchain vault that makes thousands of copies of itself similar to how DNA does in our bodies.

In a real way, dogs and other animals invented banking millions of years ago. Anyone who's seen a dog warily carry some valuable morsel or a bone to a secret burial location, presumably to make a deposit, gets the sense they are banking it for later withdrawal. Spiders and alligators and many creatures likewise store food in safe places. Perhaps one of the most famous, the ever busy squirrel, illustrates banking at its finest, *squirreling* away a cache of nuts for winter. So in a sense, a bank is anywhere secure we put valuables for safekeeping and though we humans have formalized it into an institution, it's not fundamentally much different than what other animals do.

Regardless of how it's managed or stored, money is still *very imaginary*.

The Mint: Where Imaginary Money Is Materialized

Something magical happens at a mint. Cosmic Resources are stamped into coins and printed out on paper at a breakneck rate, literally making cash from scratch out of raw materials. Something tangible is created to *represent* something intangible. We accept these tokens of imaginary units to the point where we can then use them to buy tangible goods and services and even move mountains. This illustrates the raw power of imagination and makes one believe that the entire Universe may be imagined after all!

Even so, once the imaginary value bubble crashes for a given currency and it enters a phase of hyperinflation, it can't be printed fast enough to fulfill the expected exchange rate for goods which leads to the wheelbarrows of useless cash for a loaf of bread. The irony here is that the value of the barrow of paper and ink *is* more valuable in terms of Cosmic Resources than the loaf of bread.

In asfar as mints can be used to create collectable objects, an automated mint may have some purpose in the future but it is doubtful since 3-D printers or replicators could presumably do the same job and create such things on demand.

Interest: Imaginary Money Will Be Worth More Later

Interest had its historical origins in the lending of livestock or seeds that would then be multiplied, resulting in a surplus over the original loan and thus to repay the favor some of this surplus would be returned to the lender in good faith. However, once money was tokenized, this practice was frowned upon in certain cultures as *usury*. Money is both a record of imagined past value and a projection of future imaginary value. An obsession with money leads people down some strange paths creating elaborate systems of Interest, Credit, Insurance and Hedging where the Future value of things is predicted. Remember the Primary Cosmic Resource, Time? Yes, it turns out this has the biggest influence on money. Any money created by time, will increase to a value and then time will destroy this value, absolutely. However, during the life of the money, games are played with the changing value and a form of imaginary mining is enacted to extract value for certain players of the game. Games are fun and make good stories but not everybody is a protagonist in these stories.

To set a standard for a baseline acceptable interest rate, countries set what is referred to as the Prime Rate. This rate is used when lending money to those with good credit. In the US, one lower rate is called the Federal Funds Rate used between banks. On top of this base rate, lenders can create Terms regarding how fast interest accrues, how often it is compounded and minimum payments. This is the basis of Credit Cards which are known to have ridiculously high rates, verging on loan shark levels in some cases. The justification for interest is not based in concrete reality as it was with the livestock example above because 1's and 0's in a database don't breed that I know of.

Charging Interest is one of the most ridiculous of all ripoffs we widely accept as normal. You transfer some imaginary bits and bytes over to my account and by doing so you have the right to demand back from me an equal transfer plus an additional amount, though you have not actually done anything in the meantime other than exist and go about your business. This would not be a big problem if it weren't for the fact that this simple transaction has been known to ruin individuals, families and entire nations and drive them into bankruptcy. And if you don't make your payment in time on this additional amount, your Credit Score goes down making it harder to operate in the future. It's no surprise that this practice is outlawed by many religions as *usury*, but justified by others to the point where in fact it is common practice around the world. *There will be no Interest in the Future.*

Inflation: The Negative Interest on Living

Have you ever wondered why it cost a nickel to see a movie in the 20's but it's nearly $20 in the future we live in? For whatever reason, we've decided that things must always rise in price, never stabilize, never go down. Sure, we can point to causes of supply and demand and rising production costs but that leads us right back to the labyrinth of pyramids we found when examining the original value of money. We've decided that money is worth less as time passes so we need more for the same things, 400 times more in the case of movies. This clearly illustrates the arbitrary/imaginary nature of money and it begs the question where does it end? Do movies go up 400 more times in the next 100 years, making them $8,000 and then in 2220 they will be $3.2 million each? We can be thankful Nature doesn't work this way and has stabilized all of its pricing to zero dollars.

Whatever the cause, Demand-Pull or Cost-Push, inflation will have no role in the Cosmic Age because production will have no cost and demand will always be balanced with need. Inflation is another welcome victim of the non-monetary ecosystem.

Credit: The Imaginary Rating System

Credit, or your ability to borrow, is something one can accumulate through good financial behavior, i.e. paying debts on time. The higher your credit, the more you can borrow. To make it easier, financial overlords have devised something called a Credit Score, a number that determines your creditworthiness with respect to all manner of borrowing money: obtaining loans, credit card limits and rates, financing durable goods and property, etc.

For this system to work, it requires the full chain of imaginary money to be upheld from treasury to bank to lender. By doing so it ensures that those with low credit will struggle to operate materially much more than those with high credit, regardless of how wealthy they might be in other domains of life such as physical, genetic, mental or spiritual wealth.

Scholarships and Grants are a form of Mental Credit where one can trade assets of academic achievement for assets of tuition.

Social Credit is a strong form of credit in that one accrues more of it by doing good deeds or being a good citizen. This may turn out to be very useful in the future and is already used in many instances. However, there is a subjective aspect to determining what merits social credit and there is also potential for abuse. In China, for instance, the have employed cameras with facial recognition to watch citizens in daily activities such as where and when the cross the road. Those that obey the laws garner social credit points and begin to enjoy benefits that others with lesser scores don't. Such systems don't necessarily take into account that there was no traffic when they crossed and that they were saving time.

We already do and can even greater use of a credit system in the future applied beyond the mundane of only material things. For example one could garner credit likewise in any other the identified wealth and ancillary wealth types:

Social Credit: A score for how beneficially one operates with others in society

Mental Credit: Grades, test scores, degrees and proof of knowledge. Not all mental credit is awarded by schools but is also earned in life through experience over time.

Genetic Credit: This is probably the original credit system as animals picked mates and the fittest survived in a Darwinian sense.

Physical Credit: Fitness and health are great examples of gaining physical credit which has direct benefits in other areas of life and improves the quality of life.

Spiritual Credit: Good karma is a form of spiritual credit.

When Everything is Free, Everybody is Wealthy

What if everything were free? Food, buildings, land, water, energy—everything. This seems silly in our materialist, capitalist society but from what was written above one can at least entertain the idea that the price we put on material things is somewhat arbitrary. So let's imagine zero cost. No work. No labor. No cost. All you have to do is live your life. Then the question becomes how does one live such a life as a freeloader? This is a real and difficult question to answer. It is human nature to seek purpose in our days. We currently fill our days providing for ourselves and our families but what if everything was provided by our hypothetical and very plausible auxons? What then would we fill our days with and how would we share free things with one another? Because if it's free for you and free for them, then sharing isn't even a big deal, very much like we share the free air we breathe. To enjoy such a life, one needs to accrue a far more important sort of wealth— *Mental Wealth*.

If everybody is materially wealthy, then *nobody is* and the dichotomy of haves and have nots becomes just *haves*. It becomes dull and pointless to speak of one's wealth when the exact same wealth belongs to any other person. In many ways, this is already the case but we don't allow ourselves to know it yet.

Unlike previous Revolutions that relied on dismantling or reining in the ruling class to solve large social inequities, this rEvolution solves the problem in reverse, turning the underclass into material equals of the ruling class. So no wealth is taken away from the haves, but only given to the have nots. There is some likelihood that the standard of living for even the most materialistic rich person could be elevated also in the process.

The Guises and Perils of Greed

Greed can be said to be an overzealous desire to possess the assets of one or another type of wealth. Entertaining a personal fantasy or having a daydream is generally fairly harmless. However, the illusion of wealth and ownership leads entire masses of humanity mindlessly around by the nose and the mechanisms of Capitalism in particular operate so far out of the laws of biology and physical reality that they threaten our very existence. One of the most counter-nature parts of the Capitalism is the almighty Return on Investment (ROI). Shareholders have come to expect year on year growth of 10% or greater and companies will do almost anything to provide that.

Most commonly they will try:

Lower quality (use cheaper materials or shoddier manufacturing but charge the same or more)
Reduce labor costs
Spend more on marketing (create more false needs)
Expand domain (eg. Fish in more places with bigger nets)
Mergers and acquisitions
Automate more
Raise prices
Cut regulations
Lower taxes

Now these all seem perfectly normal in business and we have allowed this to become the norm to an every-increasing extent, regularly praising companies for meeting or exceeding expectations. However, it's not sustainable in many cases. So often, profits are geared toward short-term goals and the long-term is swept under the rug with "we'll figure it out later." This runs into a hard wall eventually, one that is built by ancient biology and a finite Biosphere on a finite, closed-system Planet. *Consequences of unregulated growth are not unlike cancer*, which is unregulated growth in the body. We are so enamored of this system that we will let companies who *pretend* to own Cosmic Resources, for example, oil, and sell it all over the world, including to support unregulated military activity and proceed to alter the chemistry of our Atmosphere. Or, on a personal level, we freely allow pharmaceutical companies to pursue drugs that will either create lifelong dependencies or withhold cures because it would threaten the ROI for investors. So we have a system founded on a huge conflict of interest between profitability and doing what is right and what will lead to less suffering, both physically and financially. Of course, if these companies were guided by higher principles and could learn to live sustainably within our means, we wouldn't all be vulnerable to extinction at worst and misery at best in the name of Greed for more, more, more.

Greed eventually leads to conflict, often in the form of extreme violence, including war.

Can greed be good too? What of greed for other types of wealth? Let me list some pros and cons next to each type and encourage the reader to think of more examples:

Type of Greed	Pros	Cons
Physical	Quest for longevity or better health	Quest for physical immortality or physical domination over another, narcissism.
Mental	Is a thirst for knowledge different than a greed for knowledge? How much is too much knowledge.	Perhaps one would shirk other responsibilities in society of family in the greedy pursuit of knowledge.Self-obsession, narcissism. Lack of rest, overstimulation, loneliness.
Genetic	Cure for diseases	Designer babies and clones
Material	Philanthropy, charity	Hyper-materialism, gluttony
Spiritual	Spiritual leadership and exemplary life, altruism	Monastic, overly inward

Conflict of Interest: When Greed Collides With Need

A Conflict of Interest arises when a party working toward a certain goal has an ancillary goal to satisfy as well and where satisfying both goals is impossible as one goal may preclude the achievement of the other. The most pervasive and impactful example of this can be found in our Healthcare System but there are endless examples. For example, if one's goal is to find a cure for a particular malady AND to maximize one's profit in doing so it can quickly lead to a situation where it is less profitable to cure the malady[12]. Take Diabetes. Selling a lifetime supply of needles, blood measuring devices, insulin and other drugs as well as all the attendant products and services of associated maladies like obesity, amputations, etc. produces far more revenue than a one time cure would produce so the business is de-incentivized to produce the cure. Or, if a cure or excellent treatment does not involve expensive, FDA approved pharmaceuticals but instead could be as well or better treated with readily available nutrition/diet changes or cheaply produced natural remedies, it won't garner the research money to prove the efficacy because in the end, not enough imaginary money will be gained.

---

[12] https://www.cnbc.com/2018/04/11/goldman-asks-is-curing-patients-a-sustainable-business-model.html

The Government is filled with such conflicts of interest where the needs of the many are superseded by the needs of the few. And because we have a powerful Senatorial Body where small populations are represented at the same level as large populations, the small populations can lord over the large ones in ways that conflict with the needs of tens of millions of people vs. the needs of thousands, even when the needs of the larger population coincide with those of the smaller population that doesn't understand it or wants to go its own way regardless of reason. In fact, the Government is one big conflict machine almost rarely doing what is in the actual interest of the Nation in order to satisfy various factions within.

Not all conflicts of interest derive from greed but rather from circumstance. Lawyers and therapists and all sorts of professions often need to recuse themselves from cases or patients where it could create a conflict of violate the rights of another client or patient. Such conscientious deconfliction indicates a much higher mindset compared to the greed-driven decision to place corporate shareholder returns above the needs of patients or citizens.

Extreme Wealth Through the Lens of Absurdity

Sometimes it helps to analyze things entirely regarding how absurd they seem and how disproportionate and downright bizarre they appear. This serves the purpose to diminish the validity of taking the absurd thing seriously. Extreme wealth and extreme greed are ripe for such analysis, especially when put in a Natural context. For example, let's say we live on average 80 years x 365 days x 3 meals per day = 87,600 meals in a lifetime (counting the breastfeeding). If we paid $100 dollars for each meal, it would add up to $8.7 million. So a billionaire, having paid top dollar for each meal of life, would still have $991 million left to spend. Or let's say they paid $10 per meal, they could then afford over 1,000 lives worth of food. In Nature, this would be like a lion that hoarded 1000 times the food it could possibly eat, which is absurd. And we have humans who have tens of billions, multiplying this absurdity.

If someone with 1 billion dollars gets a reasonable 5% return on their money annually, they accrue $50 million dollars (which may be taxed) for no activity other than existing (oh, they did call their broker and opened some envelopes, we mustn't forget). This is a very decent wage of $5,707 dollars/hr., including sleep and weekends! We have individuals who do much better, at 10% return and 50 billion dollars, garnering near $500,000 per/hr. 24 hours per day by breathing. If we ever get our first trillionaire, these wages will rise to 10's and 100's of millions per hour. That is absurd.

This sort of preposterous overabundance in the Cosmic Age would be so unnecessary and moot that it simply won't exist, along with the money itself.

Let's Be Fair

We see so much hand wringing over minimum wage, the lowest acceptable pay per hour for a worker. Yet we seldom hear about maximum wage, the highest acceptable pay. Why not? The upper limit appears to be infinity if you can get it. We all know the fellow who changes bedpans at the hospital or digs the ditches works just as hard as the broker or the CEO, if not harder. We are extremely impressed with entrepreneurial success such as we see with Bill Gates, Steve Jobs,

Jeff Bezos and others. But if we fairly examined the causes of their success we find a series of unlikely events and episodes of pure luck as well as the inheritance of all the things society has done to enable it. Take Amazon, started as an online bookseller. However, if the government hadn't created ARPANET and then others create the Internet and others invent HTML, all the wiring, modems, routers and computers to do the work on and the teachers Mr. Bezos had growing up, Amazon could never exist. This barely covers the thousands of things that had to fall in place of the course of Mr. Bezos life. One car accident or even a wrong turn and an entirely different outcome. Yes, timing is everything and being first has its advantages but it's 99.999% luck and .001% talent if we are honest. That talent is fantastic and helps us take advantage of luck but without it, nothing can happen. There were probably a million people born every bit as talented as Mr. Bezos the same year but most of them were probably born in circumstances much less conducive to success or didn't meet the right people or have access to books, etc.

Basically, we reward good luck and punish bad luck and we cloak luck in the disguise of talent, which is unfair to those with talent who are not as lucky. Any success of an individual must be attributed at least in part to the society they live in that enables it. Society does claim its share of success in the form of taxes but it far undervalues itself as the progenitor of success. This is why, *temporarily,* wealth taxes and marginal taxes must be much higher—for fairness and to give society what it has rightfully earned. Once society can determine a proper maximum wage, insuring the opulence and philanthropic beneficiaries of wealth overabundance, then proper tax rates can be determined, until they are rendered obsolete. So many fiscal problems can be solved by this simple realization. This is very important during the transition to the Cosmic Age because in that time, Society will need great capital expenditures to create the Provisional Systems that can create lasting, sustainable wealth for all inhabitants of Earth. Society will not own these systems for those belong to the Cosmos so if it were to be called an *ism* it would be Cosmism.

Today's Poverty Is Yesterday's Wealth

There are so many examples of things that the modern person enjoys that not only couldn't exist in the past, but if they did, would be considered the stuff of kings or wizards. Running hot water, televisions, phones, computers, microwaves, air conditioners, plumbing, shaving cream, deodorants, feminine care products, painkillers, antibiotics, surgery, anaesthesia, sleeping pills, boner pills, cars, trucks, motorcycles, paved roads, supermarkets, Internet, Amazon, drones, lights, stoves, refrigerators, dishwashers, airplanes, and so much more we take for granted. Even in today's world, due to technological advances, a modern economy model is far fancier and better equipped than yesteryear's deluxe model. A 2018 Honda Civic is far more advanced than a 1955 Mercedes Benz or Rolls Royce. A 2018 iPhone is so much better than a 1990's brick phone. A 2018 $1000 computer is far more powerful than a multi-million dollar room-sized computer of the 1950's.

Moore's Law states that computing power doubles approximately every 18 months. Yes, based on clever human mental activity, this has been largely the case but because the price does not double and remains fairly constant or even lowers, the value proposition of computers is rising geometrically. Taken to its extreme, this would lead to absurdly powerful supercomputers for pennies on the dollar. As their size also shrinks, supercomputing will become ubiquitous so that even a toothbrush might contain a more powerful computer than was available to crack the Enigma code during WW2. Such a toothbrush could analyze your health and vibrate freshly minted classical music into your teeth as you brushed.

If one extrapolates this process to its logical conclusion, we end up with the best things for no cost or at least very good things for a much lower cost. This shows you that the real value comes from the mind and not the ground. It is only when we apply our minds that we improve the processes, add efficiencies and lower the cost. There seems to be no known limit to how much our minds can lower costs and improve things. Take medicine, for example. Treating a patient with cancer with expensive surgeries, chemotherapy and radiation and recovery could easily be replaced in the future with a "shot" that easily cured the cancer and cut out all the other expensive steps. Sure, because of patents, the initial cost of such a shot could be arbitrarily high but as patents expire, generics are created and competition takes over, the cost comes way down. And the real cure is free because auxons can eventually make the "magic" serum with no human labor.

Cars will become so advanced very soon that they drive themselves, essentially a human delivery system. And thus the concept of car ownership will make less and less sense because who wants a car taking up space when what you actually want is a car when you need it? Cars on demand will be the norm and they will be flying cars too!

Life in the 1800's, even if you lived in a mansion was cold, smelly, lonely, dark at night, dangerous if you got sick and you generally died by 50. Now, a poor person living in a small house has a phone, access to a clinic, lights at night, flushing toilets. What has changed? The ingenious human mind has changed the human condition in ways that can't be priced out. What's 30 more years of life worth? The Future will only come at us faster from here out. Changes will accelerate and by the time the 22nd Century arrives, the 1900's and the 2000's will seem quaint and arduous in comparison. Andrew Carnegie noted the general improvement of baseline conditions over the centuries as proof the capitalism was good.

Even when we compare poor people from one nation to another, there can be stark differences. A poor person in America is generally far wealthier than one living in the slums of Calcutta or starving in remote Ethiopia. So material wealth is currently somewhat *relative*. This relativity can be applied locally, at a national level or internationally depending on what one wants to know about the poverty. As I stated earlier, mental wealth can in some instances overcome lack material wealth so it's important not to compare apples to oranges when investigating differences. There could be entire neighborhoods in materially wealthy America where the houses are big but the occupants feel small, need all sorts of pills and are generally unhappy so it would seem somewhat of an impoverished area in regards to mental wealth.

Profit: The Magical Gain in Value

Businesses run on profits, i.e. financial gains. Buy *this* at one price, do something with it, charge more than you paid by selling *this* as *that*. The difference, minus your costs in *doing something*, is your profit, what you have gained in the doing. Profits are garnered in numerous ways including:

Trading goods from market to market—buying for less in one market and selling in another where the value is higher. eg. buy cloth in Indonesia, sell it in the US

Buying wholesale, selling retail—buying a larger quantity at a lower unit cost and selling it at a higher unit cost in smaller quantities

Manufacturing—adding labor and expertise to various input materials, outputting products to be sold for more than the cost of goods and labor input.

Artistry—a type of manufacturing, where the expertise applied is artistic in nature, eg. turning raw canvas and paints into something far more valuable.

Services—providing a valuable enough service that the cost of acquiring the skills and tools to perform it is less than what others are willing to pay for it over time

Investing—buying a share of a business and partaking of the profit and loss of the business or enterprise. This category has so many variations that an entire book could be dedicated to such things as: options, shorting, hedging, venture capital, private equity, derivatives, etc.

Mergers and Acquisitions—increasing the net worth of a company by acquiring the assets of another

Arbitrage—buying one currency and converting into another with a more favorable momentary valuation

Collecting or Holding—buying an item or a set of items that become more valuable over time due to greater rarity or demand. This can include real estate holdings.

Theft—gaining property without buying it or running a confidence game, pyramid scheme or other such con and selling it and/or stealing money from con targets. Bait and switch is a common con in which the seller fools the buyer into thinking the thing purchased is more valuable than it is by means of deception. Extortion and blackmail are also ways in which detrimental or derogatory information is leveraged to extract a profit from the target. There are nearly no limits to the ways humans have devised for stealing from one another.

Gambling—investing/betting money on a random process where the odds of losing the money exceed the odds of gaining a profit

The opposite of profit is *loss* or net negative gain. Loss has numerous causes including:

Foolishness
Bad luck
Bad timing
Misinformation
Mismanagement
Theft
Laziness
Procrastination

Poor judgement
Delusion

Over time, if losses exceed profits, debt, bankruptcy or receivership ensues. If on the other hand profits exceed losses, the enterprise is said to be *profitable*.

No matter by what means one gains a material profit, it will always be imaginary because no net change has taken place that one can fully claim. You didn't change the quantity of Cosmic Resources but only shifted their position in space and time. In many case, nothing other than bits and bytes were moved around in a closed circuit such as with day traders or hedge fund managers. The state of the trading system, barely any different physically, yet produced an imaginary profit composed of imaginary money that no one can tell you where it actually is. But the good news is that the *losses are also imaginary* and what you have actually lost is an elaborate, imaginative game. That's magical.

But remember, we have four other types of wealth to profit with so all is not lost! Nothing says we can't enjoy a physical profit or a mental or spiritual profit, not to be confused with a prophet, mind you. Even a *genetic profit* can be "earned" in the way of a child who bears better traits than either parent by combining the best of one ancestry with the best of another. One could even conjecture that Evolution itself rewards genetic profits with survival.

So for completeness let's take a look at what we might call profit and loss in the other wealth types:

Physical Profits: Growing of plants and animals, cleaning of water and air producing better health, better health, healing a wound, exercise, diverting an asteroid bound for Earth.

Genetic Profits: A child with better traits than the parents, a species that survives extinction, a mutation of a gene that leads to a better organism

Mental Profits: Reading a book that leads to a unique insight, listening to music that inspires joy, educating oneself to have a fulfilling career and life, training to become a black belt or other forms of mastery, seeing a therapist and improving your mental health

Spiritual Profits: A gain in karma by doing good deeds (mitzvah in Judaism), an answered prayer, communing with Nature or meditation producing a sense of connectedness and inner well-being, holiness, Good, Heaven[†]

Likewise, we can experience loss in all of these areas as well:

Physical Loss: Loss of health, amputation, pollution, degraded environment, an asteroid striking the Earth, aging, death

Genetic Loss: A child who regresses by inheriting worse traits than the parents, a mutation of a gene that is detrimental to the individual or the species

Mental Loss: Becoming unhappy or depressed, mental illness, apathy and loss of cognitive interest, forgetting things you once knew

Spiritual Loss: Bad karma for doing bad deeds, negative prayers wishing bad to come on others, disrespect for the holy, unholiness, Evil, Hell[†]

Thinking these things up is sort of an interesting diversion in itself and the reader is encouraged to think of other ways in which we might profit besides the usual ones. The only rule is that we end up with something greater or better than we started with by *wisely using our time*. No matter, it requires time to gain a profit.

Often, a "profit" is gained at the expense of another or even at the expense of the World. Most profit calculations are far from truthful or complete. For example, one may find it is far more profitable to dump some toxic byproduct of a manufacturing process into a conveniently located river or dump site. After all, it's expensive to handle toxic waste. So, even though the company has boosted the bottom line, they have passed all manner of costs on to society and reaped an undeserved artificial reward. In the short video, The Story of Stuff,[13] the narrator shows us a more truthful look at the full cycle involved in manufacturing—the true costs. An example from the video, for every truck of goods delivered to Walmart and other such retailers, approximately 17 trucks worth of garbage are created in the process! Another way to put this common flaw of modern capitalism is the *profit is privatized and the liability is socialized*.

† No claim is made as to the existence of Heaven and Hell, but to say that we may all have some model of Final Spiritual Destination and it varies from culture to culture, religion to religion. One might say that one destination is Good and the other is Bad, Reward and Punishment, Existence and Non-existence, In the Book of Life, Out of the Book of Life. Heaven and Hell can be found right here on Earth for many.

Preposterous Overcharging

One can run another thought experiment to see how preposterous and bully-like overcharging or even charging at all for what the Cosmos has provided free of charge. Imagine that we get to a place where everything is ticking along with free solar energy in a beautiful green world. We've mastered the hurdles of energy storage so we can enjoy plentiful power all through the night and day. Suddenly, during the height of the day, everything goes dark. We get a transmission from a superior being who has installed a very large high-tech shutter between the Earth and the Sun who demands large sums of gold or some other form of payment for us to continue receiving the sunlight. The being doesn't even have to threaten our destruction because soon the Earth would start to freeze over without the solar energy. We would be forced to either pay or go to war with a civilization that is clearly far, far ahead of us or roll over and die. We'd likely start to pay the extortion money. While this is far fetched, it's very similar to what many Earthlings do to each other daily— those in power lord over those without the power simply because they can. We have created a shake down system where landlords and shareholders have their way. We live with daily extortion.

Out of water and air, two molecular essentials for life, one has already been fully commercialized and it seems like a matter of time before air is charged for and bottled up. As soon as *they* figure it out.

---

13 https://www.youtube.com/watch?v=9GorqroigqM

The Ripoff Society

This phase of capitalism can be referred to as the Ripoff Society. *In the Ripoff Society, anything that can be charged for will be charged for.* Whatsmore, the charge will increase over time and the deliverable will be reduced. Also, marketing in the Ripoff Society is deceitful because telling a lie allows sellers to boost profits (increase amount of ripoff) by duping more buyers. A simple example of this is seen with the proliferation of fake reviews, where the seller has paid to have positive reviews of their product by those that never owned it, yet boosting sales marginally. And we see little white lies and omissions in advertising all the time.The Ripoff Society is essentially a mechanism of stealing time from other people in the form of money that they work for using theirs and others' time. Any time the cost of an item rises beyond the base inflation rate, it's likely because of the Ripoff Society, not for any real need.

Viewing people as mere quantifiable consumers with no attendance to the qualitative state of being human has allowed companies to continuously make life more expensive and less satisfying.

Of course, this will all turn out to be an ignorant phase of a society that has no actual purpose or meaning other than to blindly consume and extract time from others for no good purpose.

Entropy: The Greatest Rip Off Artist

Entropy is a fact of Reality—the tendency of things to chaotically move about and bounce of another and fly apart. Life, on the other hand, is sort of *Extropic* in nature and tends to organize (organism) and put things neatly in place. These two forces are at constant odds with each other, often in the service of life. As the bees make their perfect honeycombs, the bear seeks to rip it apart and eat the honey. In a sense, the bear has stolen the time from the bees that they took to construct the honeycomb.

And humans are no different, in fact much worse. We regularly steal time from each other and we do it all day every day, often in meaningless ways. Modern life has only accelerated and amplified what was once a natural survival tendency and put it into our lives in ways that have no intrinsic value. A perfect example of this is spam emails or phone calls. Every time you take action to look at your phone or delete incoming spam messages, you have used up some of your finite Time Resource. Or rather, it has been stolen from you. This crime is so egregious and taken on a whole, it costs humanity centuries of man-hours of lost time. Once one understands the value of time, then one must conclude that spammers are to be punished severely until they no longer exist. However, achieving that through punishment is not nearly as perfect as through obsolescence.

Entropy can be commercialized. We are bombarded with advertisements throughout our lives, consuming years of time on things you will never buy and certainly don't need. Even in less nefarious ways, entropy plagues us in dime and nickel ways. Every time your computer or phone asks you if you are ready to update or, God forbid, you actually decide yes, it's time to update, a smaller or larger slice of your time on Earth will go poof! And this can quickly cascade into a whole series or further updates of no longer compatible software, drivers, etc., or even worse, be a poor update that degrades the performance of your device, stealing even more future time from you, all in the friendly guise of progress.

Governments can be the biggest Entropic villains, wasting billions or trillions of dollars worth of labor and materials—*and time.* One poor decision can lead to a monumental cascade of wasted effort. Great examples of this can be found in the building of large walls such as the Great Wall of China, the Berlin Wall and possibly a large, Nature-killing proposed wall on the US Southern border.

Not only can entropy can be weaponized, it often is the weapon itself. What is a bomb but a tool to scramble up organized matter into chaos or a gun to scramble up the insides of a body? Too much entropy is not a good thing for life. On a more subtle level, entropy can also be used to scramble up society. When you look at the results of social media tampering to sow and amplify divides among the populus, what you are witnessing is a "stirring of the pot." Creating false narratives not only wastes people's time but causes them to then bounce into others, wasting their time as well. The perpetrator however is like the bear with the bees and getting what is desired.

One of the many positive outcomes of a Materially Satisfied world, is there would be no need to fish for dollars or suckers because we'd already have everything we need. But even well before that, AI will learn to squash spam (it already can) before it ever reaches you, no matter how cleverly disguised it is.

But make no mistake, Entropy will eventually disintegrate you and scatter your ashes to the wind, so don't get *too* attached to your physical body or those of your loved ones.

A self-maintaining Auxonic System is the ultimate extropic fighter in the war against Entropy. But entropy is not a foe that can ever be fully defeated since it is built into the fabric of space-time and is needed for life and even matter to operate normally.

Prison: Time Used As Punishment

Prison is a construct we have created to actively erase/remove time from an individual's life, or more precisely, the freedom of how to spend that time. We often say "doing time" with regards to prison. This illustrates that we very much value time and that to take it away is one of our harshest punishments. The Death Penalty is our way of taking away all Earthly time for an individual. *You don't do time. Time does you.*

Superior prison systems seek not to destroy and waste the inmate's time but rather to utilize it to rehabilitate, educate and foster a better chance that the prisoner will emerge as a more prepared citizen and not return to the offending behavior. This is an Extropic approach rather than Entropic, seeking to "organize" the prisoner's time for the greater good of society. The time will pass regardless. How one uses it is all that matters.

But you don't have to be sent to prison in order for "the system" to steal some of your time. Every time you wait at a stop light when there is no traffic, a little bit of you goes into the void. Commuting and work itself is a theft of time to greater or lesser degree, depending on how lucky you are. For many, work is another form of prison. Anyone who has worked at a company that requires one to use a punch-clock upon arrival and leaving and administrative "punishment" that results from even the slightest unexplained tardiness understands this feeling. Fortunately, we can use that commuting time to increase our mental and spiritual abundance if we choose to so it need not be time wasted.

The Intersection of Material and Mental Wealth: Intellectual Property

One of humanity's greatest abilities is invention. To invent something, you have to possess mental wealth. You have to understand a need and have sufficient creativity to dream up a new way to do something and often, need to be fairly well educated to do so. Nevertheless, society has agreed that this exceptional achievement only deserves so much credit and thus patents are only good for about 20 years and copyrights for about 75. After that, the idea becomes public domain. So in the longer arc of history, ALL ideas are eventually public domain, no matter how grand. This is for a good reason though it might not be thought of this way—you didn't invent that alone. You had parents or guardians who fostered you, you had folks building roads and computers you used. You had teachers and more and all these things added up to enable you to invent something, often relying on prior art or a previous invention. Nothing happens in a vacuum. Even the innate skills you possess as a genius inventor you owe to your genetic heritage and the circumstances of your childhood.

A large, trillion dollar corporation such as Apple, pays thousands of people imaginary money to file dozens of patents every day. Each patent is ingenious in some way, no doubt. However, in many ways, these patents belong to all of humanity every bit as much as they belong to Apple. In fact, all of that imaginary money they use came from the world. We bought their goods with our imaginary money, which are all made of Cosmic Resources (silicon, metal, oil, energy, etc.) and cheap labor. If they could, they would, in a heartbeat, use free labor at an automated solar-powered plant. What company wouldn't want workers who were super precise and fast, worked three shifts for no pay and no benefits and never complained, all powered with free energy from the Sun? That's a capitalist's dream, zero or little production cost and the ability to sell for a ridiculous price and garner a ridiculous profit ad infinitum. But as we know, nothing lasts forever and so after a time, such a system would necessarily lead to free products as stated above, intellectual property notwithstanding.

Further, with Artificial Intelligence (AI), it is now perfectly feasible to imagine quantum computers that can invent things much faster than humans and more complex and more ingenious in functionality than flesh and blood could ever invent. Some may call such meta-inventions the property of the software programmer that created the program that started to write its own better programs but even this is a losing cause since that original patent or copyright has a relatively short shelf life.

To summarize the genesis and life cycle of intellectual property we can break it into three phases:

The inventive phase where some protection is afforded to the inventor, upon request since nothing prevents an inventor to donate the invention for the betterment of society. Since the need for monetary reward will be removed, this may be a common approach.

The protected phase where some form of reward is transferred to the IP owner. This phase is generally a period of 20 years for patents and 75 years for Copyrights. This phase may become obsolete or be more in the form of Social or Historical Accreditation.

The public phase where the IP is committed to the Public Domain and is freely usable.

Art: The Intersection of Spiritual, Mental and Material Wealth

While the skills of an artist require all forms of wealth in concert, the Art Product is only valuable as long as it is appreciated. Some art is very temporal and loses its meaning and appreciation rapidly, often intentionally so. I and my artist brother, Michael, created a program I called DNA (Dynamic Non-Repeating Art) to create art randomly based on thousands of algorithms I had collected over time. It drew new expressive faces in an organic, artistic way ad infinitum. If you liked one of the drawings, too bad, it would soon die forever and be replaced by another. It was a metaphor for life itself and a conceptual work. I later created Art Fountain for the purpose of "permanently" capturing these works in a pure, mathematical form that is theoretically eternal but you still need a place to store and preserve these files so the value is questionable at best and zero at worst.

I mention DNA and Art Fountain, not to toot my own artistic or programming horn, but to toot the horn of conscious beings everywhere! So, even though a computer can create using algorithms and random numbers, a fairly intricate work of art, in a way, automating the art creation process, the computer doesn't get to decide if in fact it is art, we do. It's not art if there is no one to see it, touch it, taste it, smell or hear it, etc.—perceive it. As such, I "throw away" much more art than anyone will ever know because I decided it had zero value to me as the editor and artist. The process is iterative, takes time and lots of artistic decision-making.

This says a lot about our role in the Future and our ultimate value in an automated world. We are the ultimate deciders and purveyors because we possess *conscious discretion*. We also can become the meta-controllers of artistic automation by controlling the parameters used artistically. However, this is only one medium of art, i.e. algorithmic art, and each other medium establishes its own limitations based on skill, vision and physical conditions and materials.

Art has numerous media it acts on including:

Light, analog and digital
Video, both fixed form and generative
Sculpture, both fixed and dynamic such as mobiles
Pigments on a surface material
Virtual, immersive and 3-D

Art's temporal modality can include:

Ephemeral, temporary art including randomly generated

Time-limited, art that expires after a fixed period
Permanent, long-term art on long-lasting media
Archival, long-term art that can be regenerated indefinitely in the future

The longevity of art's appreciation depends on how deep the artist's inspiration was, the materials used, the good fortune of preservation and so much more. The great artists reach through Eons when they have tapped into something greater than the Physical Plane and can touch a part of our being that longs for meaning, a sense of awe and the Source of Beauty. Thus Art is the highest form of temporal Material Wealth we can possess and even the most beautiful and majestic art such as the Earth itself won't last forever but it will likely outlast Picasso.

Art has numerous important roles to play, now and forever:

To inspire	To imitate
To instruct	To remember or commemorate
To disturb or call into question	To exalt beauty
To calm or comfort	To decorate
To warn	To entertain
To humor	To mystify
To mock	To beautify
To frighten	To enlighten

Time: The Priceless Treasure We Give Away

How much is our time worth? Depending on who you ask, it's 40¢/month in North Korea, $7.15/hour in some states and hundreds of thousands per day for some CEO's. We almost always put the value of time into wages when in fact it has nothing to do with them. If you ask a philosopher what time is worth, you may have to first prove that time exists. One thing we can agree on is that, on average, we are given more or less 75-90 years worth to live our biological lives with the middle portion being more vivid and active, if we are lucky. As of yet, no billionaire has been able to buy much more time. Steve Jobs, the founder of Apple with access to the finest healthcare, could not another day buy at some point and passed away like every other human. Theoretically, if time were purchasable he could have traded his life fortune for 10 more years, right? He still had lots more to offer and that he no doubt was not ready to throw in the towel. But no, there is no amount of money, all the money on Earth, that can buy one more second of time when your *time* comes. Time is literally priceless, or lacking monetary value, yet we treat it as a cheap commodity worth less than a large carbon crystal (i.e. diamond).

Time is the only Cosmic Resource that dwindles on its own with no power to stop it (without entering a black hole or reaching the speed of light—whichever comes first). Your days are exactly as grains of sand in an hourglass.

As I said before, no matter what we do, the same amount of time will pass. Work all day or sit at home all day. Work out for hours or watch TV for hours. In the end, it's the Quality of Time Spent that matters—how it affects our physical, mental and spiritual wealth. If you spend all your days pursuing more money and more material wealth but lay dying with no friends and an empty feeling of powerlessness and worthlessness, you have lost everything and wasted your life, to be soon forgotten.

We commonly use the terms: *spending time*, *killing time*, *wasting time* and *time well spent*. This indicates that in truth we do value time and know it's not good to waste it. Some time *is* more valuable than other time you might spend. The time a surgeon takes to save a person's life is multiplied a thousand times by the gift of that person in the lives of their loved ones that is made possible by the surgeon. In this case, the patient is benefitting from the large amount of time the surgeon spent developing the skills required. We we watch a concert we are also benefiting from the time spent by the musicians practicing and listening to music.

As an exercise in mindfulness I would recommend to the reader to get into the habit of becoming more aware of one's time. Try to discover where you have "time leaks" that are either not fulfilling or seem wasteful or where someone or something has stolen some of your time or undervalued it. There is not always a course of action that can be taken and once time is gone it can't be recovered but often one can at least minimize certain types of time loss by being more organized. Doing nothing is *not* a waste of time, unless that's all you do. Examples of wasted time are: things that subtract from fulfillment, cause undue negative emotions, being forced to think about something you are not interested in or to take actions dictated by a disinterested third party, like deleting spam messages. I refuse to play.

Also, we must try to be mindful of how we benefit from others' time. This develops a healthy appreciation and mutual respect for our fellow beings and even for our own time. We too often take others' time for granted and don't stop to comprehend what they have given us—the most valuable gift available.

When we eat food, in a real sense, we ingest time. The food not only generally increases our own time by giving us energy, but all of the growing, production, delivery, the sunlight and other energy within the food contains a lot more time than it takes for us to eat the food for sure. Food is a great way to illustrate wasted time as well and not only because it gets thrown away so often. For example, one can take the same basic ingredients and in the same amount of time make something delicious or by doing things in the wrong order or proportions, something terrible tasting. In this case the food's potential was squandered. Many students in America suffer from this particular unnecessary shortcoming of food potential while counterparts around the world rate much higher, often on lower budgets.

Becoming more aware of time as a dwindling resource, in general, increases appreciation of life.

Taxation: Can We Have Some of Your Time?

In as far as we work for a living by receiving a paycheck for compensation, we also donate or are forced to, a certain portion of that work to *taxes*, money supposedly for government to run. We also pay a tax on top of purchases of all types in the form of sales taxes. And taxes levied by corporations are called fees instead. In most cases, a significant portion of one's life will be spent *working for the State*—coming down to many years of raw time spent. This is time you can't have back, the most valuable of all Cosmic Resources. If by some medical miracle we became immortal, the we would mathematically spend a portion of Eternity working for the State. So it's a pretty big deal if the government can operate with no cost. Then there would be no cost to pass along to taxpayers.

It's not that given our current system tax is bad or evil but that it has a huge imaginary component that is arbitrary and it's also extremely inefficient. In a moneyless society, taxation becomes obsolete along will all other monetary transfer systems.

There will always be some sort of tax in life, even if it's not monetary. One can't slip through life without donating a certain portion of one's time or knowledge to an external cause. In fact, we are so wound up about monetary taxes that we are not aware of other types of taxes we incur. Each type of wealth asset can be taxed in one way or another. We often say something was "taxing" to indicate it had exacted a toll on us, and it did. But in so paying our taxes to the community and to others we can enrich our lives and make the community we live in better. That's why paying one's monetary taxes has a certain amount of value to us no matter what because we gain benefits such as better schools, roads, fire protection and much more.

Ideally taxation would only be for real and good things but so much of it is lost to waste, corruption and an imagination-based pyramid scheme that has no real value except what we've been told. Thus the $800 toilet seat.

Chapter 3: The End of Money

Don't mourn the end of money. Recall all the terrible things it has caused us over the centuries and that it has often been referred to as "the root of all evil." Money is not our destiny. Money is not important. Money is literally nothing and one doesn't mourn nothing. On the contrary, please make sure to celebrate the passing of the great fraud, money. Rich and poor alike can rejoice together, because rich and poor will be alike in a clean new world of perfect abundance and no wanting of more will be required by any. It will make no more sense to want more than to want more Sun to burn yourself with. We will be quite content with the ubiquitous plenty.

All dreams eventually end or as George Harrison wisely sings, "All Things Must Pass." The dreamer either wakes up or dies. We are already seeing the beginning of the end of money. Even in rural China, farmers regularly pay for goods using their phones and are moving to a cashless society. The cashless society has already accepted the pointlessness of physical money. If we are going to have imaginary money dammit, we're going to move it around using ephemeral bits and bytes! Don't even bother printing it or stamping out coins, what a waste! It's a lot simpler. No more armored vehicles running around delivering money bags to and fro with uptight security. No more printing presses furiously churning our plates of bills. No more counterfeits. The jig is up. It's only a matter of time before all societies go cashless and a cashless society is the precursor to a moneyless society.

As more and more full-time careers are subsumed by automation, society will be forced to provide a minimum base salary to protect the people from destitution. Ephemeral digital money will magically appear in bank accounts out of nowhere. Eventually, even this charade of balance transfers will seem so meaningless and contrived that money will be exposed as the most pointless "substance" on Earth and will fade out of usage. Sure, we will still measure transactions and know where goods are flowing to but it won't be based on a need for profit and the almighty bottom line on a spreadsheet.

In the meantime, people will fight furiously for their rights to anonymous transactions, free of the eye of Big Brother. In China, after years of Centralized State-run economics and policies, they have become numb and even inured (or perhaps powerless) to the ever-watching eye of the state and are more likely to succumb to fully identified and recorded transactions. However, the United States is culturally far more protective of the rights of the individual and we like cash for its freedom value. This is also the allure of cryptocurrency, although because it is purely digital, it has a hidden danger of becoming tracked, surreptitiously. Only when money becomes obsolete will such a need for anonymous spending also become moot.

Once Money is gone due to absolute uselessness, we can then finally dispose of all of its applications:

Corporations	Hedge Funds
Taxation	Private Equity
Purchasing and Selling	Minting
Banking	Cash Distribution
Credit	Payroll
Lending	Deductions
Interest	Social Security
Stocks and Bonds	More

It sounds preposterous to do away with what have been a normal part of life for centuries but so were outhouses and chamber pots until we invented flushing toilets. It won't happen overnight but as it happens, the futility and pointlessness of activities surrounding a dead medium of transaction will become apparent.

There are no systems created by humans that last forever. Each runs its course and history is strewn with obsolete and extinct practices, some lasting centuries, others decades and less. To name a few:

Bloodletting, barbers bleeding patients to cure diseases
Mummification
Drinking mercury as a tonic
Lighting torches or gas lamps to light cities

Coal powered trains and boats
Trading tulips as money
Sacrificing virgins at altars
Cassette tapes, VCR's and Victorolas
Drawing and quartering and electric chairs
Ploughing by hand
Plundering and pillaging
Use of chamber pots
Trephination, making holes in skulls to let out evil spirits

Now any of these things could be revisited by a modern culture in a more enlightened way. For example, mummification has a modern variant where one is buried as an organic "seed pod" to fertilize a growing tree which serves a purpose. Blood transfusions are sort of a modern variant on bloodletting. But in general, ideas and memes run their course the same way as biological entities do so the end of money is not particularly shocking and will happen for a reason—it is no longer needed.

The idea of a society without money is neither new nor original, though people have arrived at the concept from two basic perspectives:

Isolated tribal societies that don't use money, generally living a simple if not primitive life, often using barter

Utopian concepts such as the Free World Charter[14] where we socially engineer ourselves to think differently

However, if one follows the trends and the logical results, one sees not so much a conscious choice as an evolutionary process that becomes a consequence of no longer needing money to satisfy nearly all of our needs and wants due to the abundance of Cosmic Products.

Cosmic Automation Has Many Benefits

Besides satisfying our material/physical needs, Automating certain types of work could also make the world a safer, more hospitable place. For example, instead of letting fires consume large swaths of forest, we could have robotic Firefighters that could tirelessly handle much more arduous situations and could snuff out fires before they grew out of control.

Automated AI detection of illegal weapons could stop the scourge of gun and other types of violence that has killed millions of people. Integrated into Law Enforcement, society could reach new levels of safety and security, the primary purpose of Government.

These and many similar tasks would have the effect of increasing everyone's Physical Wealth at no cost.

---

[14] http://freeworldcharter.org/en/more

A partial list of such Utility Auxons includes:

Fire and Security
Ocean cleanup
Waste processing
Toxic dump cleanup
Disaster relief
Road and bridge maintenance
Garbage and litter collection
Recycling
Forest and Wetland protection
Anti Poaching
Space cleanup

Such processes would have no daily limits or shifts and could operate tirelessly based on nearly limitless free energy, continuously improving and restoring the physical environment and enriching our lives at no cost to us*.

Besides these benefits, the free delivery of goods and food will make many annoying things obsolete that not only rob us of time but of our potential as humans. These include:

Taxation
Inflation
Advertising of all types
Spam
Online shopping
Trips to the store
Commuting
Banking
Insurance
Credit cards
Bill paying
Market trading and investment
Lottery for money
Gambling for money
Sexual harassment in corporate settings
Excessive signage on roads: smart automated vehicles don't need signs
The need to perform disingenuous, time-wasting jobs in the service of the above

There are even more monumental negative aspects of human life that could be eliminated or greatly reduced:

Endless cycles of inflation, recession, depression
Systemic Greed
Invasion of privacy for profit
Crime

Hunger and famine
Homelessness
War
Empty Materialism
Depression and anxiety

These are not as much goals of the system as the beneficial consequences of Material Programming and the obsolescence of monetary exchange.

*We could pay dearly for such auxonic helpers if we allowed them to besmirch the landscape, be ugly or overly noisy so we should proceed with this in mind.

3-D Printing, Replicators and Nanotechnology

More than robots, auxons and AI will determine the material future. The 3-D printing revolution is well on its way and it points to its eventual replacement the Replicator which will exist when we have mastered nano-scale manufacturing using billions of molecular size machines that rapidly build, atom by atom. 3-D printing does pretty well already with layer by layer but will seem primitive once the other is ready. In the meantime, we can already "print" houses by uploading a design to a large scale 3-D printer, feeding the concrete material. Not only can it create the walls, it can create the voids in the walls for wiring and plumbing, window sills, benches and it's not limited to rectilinear designs where we can can be as imaginative as we want. By extending this to the not-too-distant future, we can see that architecture will undergo its next great revolution where the most elaborate and fantastical blueprints can easily be printed into the real world with a handful of laborers. An important part of creating Mental Wealth is surrounding ourselves with beauty. An added bonus of the Free Future is that advertising will be obsolete because no one has anything to sell or convince you to buy. So our landscapes won't be ruined with large billboards and gaudy displays that create dissonance in the mind and spirit, even when we are not aware. Architecture plays a huge role in Mental Wealth. A child that grows up around beautifully designed buildings and houses will have a better attitude than one who grows up around a chaos of boxy designs, wires and billboards.

With nanotechnology, you have possibilities that go far beyond manufacturing, some quite scary such as when it is weaponized. In his book Engines of Creation[15], K. Eric Drexler builds on ideas posited by famed physicist, Richard Feynman regarding the "smallest possible machines" and the limits thereof. He lays out a scientific foundation for a revolution in manufacturing far more astounding and transformative than we saw in the Industrial Revolution or even in the *macrorobotics* that are common today. I will address weapons and warfare separately from this treatise on Wealth and Drexler himself spends a great deal of time on the danger of weaponized or even accidentally out of control nanotechnology. On the positive side, nanotechnology has the potential to cure diseases, create rockets made out of diamond and clean up the oceans. In a real sense we ourselves are the ultimate nanotechnology as our DNA and RNA and cellular machinery go about trillions of operations per day, building, protecting, healing and purifying our body on a

---

[15] http://e-drexler.com/d/06/00/EOC/EOC_Table_of_Contents.html

molecular level. To master this sort of thing requires time but the rewards are so huge we will eventually have to. With nanotechnology, one gets the most efficient form of manufacturing that requires no welding, hammering, riveting, screwing, drilling, etc. Things are built one atom at a time very rapidly and like 3-D printing, in nearly any shape or form imaginable.

Anyone who saw *Star Trek* remembers the Replicator. Imagine a sort of microwave that can also build your food, create a pair of shoes, a folded silk shirt with diamond buttons, etc. Things that would cost a fortune today, will cost next to nothing. Not only such such devices create food, but they will be able to create the most delicious and nutritious foods without torturing animals, or spraying toxins. Fresh fruit and vegetables will still be plentiful as green farms become efficient and automated and pesticide free.

There are possible limits such as the fact we can't easily manufacture Elements such as gold or platinum. Those require unimaginable energy levels and are forged by colliding Neutron Stars but we are already supplied with copious amounts of all of these elements for no charge by the Cosmos. There are large nuggets of pure gold floating around in space. Gold can certainly be thought to be priceless but so is everything else the Cosmos provides because there is no seller. Without a rightful owner and seller, no one has claim to these resources and they belong to the Cosmos.

Extraterrestrial Wealth

Do aliens exist? Are they wealthy? We know if they do exist they have inherited the same Cosmic Resources we have so they have would have done something similar in manipulating these resources into useful things such as space ships. In many ways we could discover the end game of our own thoughts and beliefs on wealth by examining beings who are far more advanced, perhaps by millions or even billions of years. What becomes of a society where everything ceased being "paid" for eons ago? Is pay a human thing only? We don't see much of it in the animal world though we know of some species that trade sex for other things.

Gene Roddenberry, the genius creator of Star Trek, did us a great favor by thoroughly exploring a future alter ego of sorts for humanity. Other science fiction writers have also imagined all manner of possible futures for humanity and distant civilizations. You never see Spock whipping out his wallet to pay for things on the Enterprise or even on most planets except when the writers wanted to highlight the primitive nature, even the absurdity of such systems.

If one were to experience a Close Encounter of seeing a UFO or its inhabitants up close, I doubt one's first thought would be, "Wow, they are so wealthy!" Yes, they are riding in a diamond craft that no amount of money on Earth could buy and possess knowledge beyond our greatest scholars, but we would tend to view them more as a natural phenomenon to be awed by than in terms of our own antiquated systems. Take note of that because we may be them sooner than you think!

One thing's sure—there are large chunks of gold, platinum and diamonds, vast amounts, floating around in space with nobody to see or claim them yet. There are all conceivable elements and compounds. Just one of these asteroid sized gold nuggets, if brought back to the Earth, could crash the gold markets here. And that is to say nothing of the unimaginable mass of gold found at the center of any planet or star, including our own.

Money Can't Buy a Dyson Sphere

Eventually, after millions and millions of years, auxons will operate on scales we can't fathom today. Like swarms of nanotech spiders, they will be able to create star-scale structures in Space that we can inhabit comfortably, harnessing the free energy of our star or other stars in the Galaxy. Manually building such a structure would be impossible and completely unnecessary. A sphere that encases a star, like the largest apartment building imaginable, is sometimes referred to as a Dyson Sphere[16] after noted theoretical physicist Freeman Dyson who posited the inevitability of such structures given sufficient evolutionary time. There is no reason for such a structure to be spherical or contiguous, only overwhelmingly, geometrically large. Scientists are currently studying several stars that are being periodically occulted by an unknown phenomenon and are wondering if this is what they are witnessing. We don't know if such things in fact exist but we can say they are theoretically possible within the Laws of Physics. So far, no Dyson Spheres have been confirmed to exist. We could simply leave it as a converse question to Feynman's smallest machine possible—what is the largest machine possible?

By this point, *homo sapiens* will be long extinct and we will be the ancient ancestors of the beings that inhabit these architectural planets and spheres. Such a civilization would have no need for money and the Dyson Sphere would become in itself a sort of ultimate Cosmic Product on a stellar scale. The materials required would be so vast as to preclude "purchase" at any but next to zero cost per cubic meter. The labor would cost nothing all powered by the star and the materials would be free all provided by original Cosmic Resources, freely mined from asteroids, moons and planets. Even working at a rapid clip, such a structure could take thousands, if not millions of years to be built.

Well before we get to the level of civilization that is building a Dyson Sphere, even soon from now, we can apply the same logic to the creation of all manner of Earthly Cosmic Products where the finest product can be produced for next to no cost on the same basis.

Regardless of when we may or may not progress to such a level, the great thinker and physicist Stephen Hawking concluded that Space is to be explored and embraced as our salvation and final frontier. No one can doubt the endless potential and vastness of Outer Space to absorb overflowing populations on Earth. In Space we can continue our story into Eternity, if the Cosmos allowed. We'd always be one stray black hole away from extinction though.

Even in the near term, we can clearly see examples of successful habitats in space such as the International Space Station. We have private companies working on commercial trips to orbit and dreaming up hotels in space and it won't be long before space towns and then space cities arrive, some orbiting, some on the Moon or Mars. We will know we are on our way to a Dyson type presence when we start building habitats orbiting the Sun instead of our planet but baby steps first.

---

[16] https://en.wikipedia.org/wiki/Dyson_sphere

Black Holes, Where Value Goes to Die (and Be Reborn)

No matter what you are, the most dense piece of Uranium or the lightest Hydrogen or the most beautiful sculpture, or shiniest Gold and Diamond Architectural Planet worth quadrillions of Earth dollars, or Red Giant, or an Entire Galaxy filled with these, once you cross over the Event Horizon of a black hole, you become beyond worthless to the outside world. All of your electrons, protons, neutron, gluons, quarks, etc. are crushed into a singularity, a single infinitesimal point in space with infinite density. The only value one might get from a black hole is as a weapon that could somehow be directed toward an enemy, even a very small one would destroy any world that came in its path. The only catch is you better have a lot of mass if you want to redirect a black hole because *they* are the ones who do the directing if you don't! Many black holes have been discovered and mapped out by astronomers, including a supermassive one at the center of our own galaxy.

A supermassive black hole is the final destination of all matter and energy and of all smaller black holes. Black holes are where all Cosmic Resources die and are no longer resources to the outside world. *A black hole is not itself a resource. However, it's gravitational effect could be used.* The only thing separating you from a black hole is time. Now the catch is, we may very well already be inside a black hole and not know it. We could very well be a hologram on the surface of a black hole so all may not be lost, except to those outside our black hole who may as well not exist.

Scientists and philosophers still don't know the fate of the Universe. Will it collapse back into a singularity in the Big Crush and start the process anew? Will it dissipate after 10 to the 100th years into a cold death? Is it a multiverse where "universes" come and go all day every day? Does any knowledge or information survive from one version of the Universe to the next? We may find that Spiritual Wealth is Eternal and not subject to the laws of matter whatsoever. We simply don't know and may never know. We do know that based on current knowledge, the Universe is in what appears to be it's infancy relative to its potential age. Give the vast scale of time, the age of the Universe could double, triple and so forth many orders of magnitude and that leaves ample time for all possible Evolution to take place.

What About All Those Great Businesses?

Think of your favorite restaurant where the food is hand crafted and served pleasantly with a great atmosphere that was carefully honed over time or maybe it's a hole-in-the wall you love. Or how about a super cool place of entertainment such as Meow Wolf in Santa Fe, New Mexico, offering unique, artistically made immersive *experiences*. Or your favorite shop or gym or whatever. What happens to all of these if all of their costs go to zero and they can no longer charge a fee for dining or admittance? No amount of robots could replace these places. In fact, they would immediately lose all of their appeal should they become automated and robotic. So how would they survive or if they thrived, how would they keep from being overrun by interested thrillseekers with no price to pay? This is where it gets interesting. All of these places tend to have one thing in common: the owners have a passion for what they are doing. By not having to pay for bookkeeping, accountants, taxes, fundraising, interest on loans, etc., these collectives of interesting, motivated people will have more time and energy to devote to pure art and craft, sparing no expense in creating the best experiences—nearly anything they can imagine. This is when the art can truly take off, when it is freed from the bonds of business.

Yes, many of them are also doing it for business reasons and to make a living but they made choices to do a particular thing that interested them. So now if we removed the component of "need to make a living" from the formula would they still be interested? Would they still be motivated to create great experiences for people or would it be too arduous when not required with that extra survival push? Let's say they were so motivated that with no urgent need, they still wanted to do it, then how would they decide who gets to come in and eat or enjoy the experience and who doesn't? As it is now, anyone who can pay the price is generally admitted, creating a natural balance between supply and demand. If the price were zero and the demand were high, the supply would be quickly outpaced.

My daughter recently attended a festival in Central Park called Global Citizen where the tickets were free to see top level music acts and high caliber speakers *IF* you qualified. Qualification required only that one volunteered to do something good for society such as registering young voters or helping with recycling or other such beneficial activities. Essentially you needed some *social credit* to attend, which is much different than money but which still required your time. Is how you spend *Time* the new money? In many ways this is more compelling than simply ponying up the cash. The attendees of Global citizen were de facto of a higher, more elevated level of citizen than if they had instead admitted anyone with the needed cash for tickets. They theoretically got a higher quality audience with shared values, making the concert a little more special for both the artists and the audience. That's one way to pay that doesn't take money and matches the supply to the demand.

Of course, there are many cases when you want a general audience for your offering. In that case, if there is a high demand, entry could be based on a lottery pick or a reservation system or the enterprise could be expanded or franchised to accommodate the demand.

Then there are the either not so great businesses and the merely OK businesses and the gigantic megacorporations. What about these? The good news is when a crappy business disappears, nobody notices except the people who worked there and since that problem will be solved in terms of material needs it won't matter much. Also, businesses are bad for many reasons, commonly poor management but also bad luck or ahead of their time (bad timing). Or they are lacking in vision or skills to execute the vision. Some businesses are terrible because they are socially detrimental or even sort of evil, like a hitman business on the dark web. Money, or should I say, *the need for money*, motivates people to do all sorts of unethical things, often not even aware of what they are doing. Such places would evaporate into thin air when the imaginary motivator was removed.

The least likely survivors of business are large corporations. Like dinosaurs, they are large lumbering organizations or people who can't possibly share a core desire to do the thing they are doing. Would you honestly want to keep working at a rental car counter if A) a robot could do your job or B) you were intrinsically wealthy. All of those bureaucratic departments would fall apart as fast as if every person in the company won the Megamillions lottery.

One irony is, some companies in existence today could very well play a huge role in their own eventual demise, such as those working on AI, machine learning and robotics. They could possibly evolve into collectives of experts that would help us navigate our way to a more utopian society and manage the complexity of the required systems.

In the end, it's not society's responsibility for us to enjoy what we are doing. It is our responsibility, so if you are doing something you don't enjoy for the sake of the thing, not the money it makes, then don't do it.

Finally, we needn't feel sorry for the loss of any business or job that is not done by desire but by necessity. If the kitchen workers disappear at your favorite Chinese restaurant and it upsets you, then you rush back there and take over the job for them. They are no longer interested and you can now get great Chinese food any time of day anyway.

Alternatives to Money as We Know It

Perhaps rather than say that money will come to an end we could also think of it as merely converting to other forms. We have seen above how social credit can be traded for other things and how one form of wealth can also be traded for another. This inter-convertability of wealth is in fact a type of exchange not unlike how we use money.

It would be dangerous to follow the path of "Social Credits" which includes negative credit or demerits. The best system would only reward tangible positive things one did toward helping society, not rewarding simple conformance to state rules.

Where Will We Live?

People work a good portion of their lives to own a home or rent it. If homes are built for free on land that belongs to the Earth, surely everybody can't have a 5 acre rolling estate, can they? Why does that guy get a better view than me? What makes him so special? They get to live in the penthouse, we're suck on the 13th floor! These are very serious problems for a society that has spent thousands of years with deeply entrenched notions of lordship over property, not to mention millions of existing homes with Titles of ownership, some going back generations within a family. Part of how we work out land/space usage in the future will greatly depend on population, terrestrial or space-based. The current system is not sustainable without a different Viability Infrastructure regarding energy usage and waste management.

We may have to develop the concept of a Stewardship Lease, where the current occupants are responsible for the well-being of the land and living quarters and are granted a lease for up to 100 years based on certain conditions being met. Some aspects will require a social credit system and other aspects a lottery not unlike the business models above. With proper stewardship, many parks and public spaces could be well-tended and enjoyed in common while everyone was guaranteed a state-of-the art living space.

Think of it another way, if you were immortal, would you live in the same place forever? That seems odd to me if one would want that. What keeps us from moving? Often it is all the possessions such as books and furniture and knick knacks and memorabilia and stuff we collect over the years. The thought of moving all to another place is daunting, not to mention prepping one's house for sale and going through all those motions. But what if *you* didn't have to move it and it cost nothing to do so or most of the same or better things could be created at your destination? Moving need be no more arduous than dragging a file from one folder to another on your computer. In this way, we might be able to enjoy many more places on the Earth, enjoying other cultures, seasons and views.

Since travel would be free, we might even lose a sense of belonging to a fixed place at all, except maybe the Earth itself. *No matter what you think about your present place, the world can always be better or as good somewhere else.* Some people may even enjoy the weightlessness of space and the majestic views of the Earth and Moon for months or even years on end, especially if one could get away for a nice trip to Greenland or somewhere exotic you had your eye on from your perch in space. Space housing would be free of the restrictions of gravitational directionally so the concept of penthouse would not really exist. Structures could be made where every home could have a spectacular view.

The actual physical living spaces of the future would have no architectural of imaginative limits because of the new building techniques using 3-D printing and nanotechnology. Furnishing could be every bit as spectacular with beautiful carpets and art and rooms that could even transform themselves. Gone would be the days of boarding up your windows for hurricanes as all of this could be automated. Upkeep and cleaning would be basically built in so people could enjoy more of their time doing things they actually wanted to do.

Because the world would be safer, we could return to a time when children could freely play outside and neighborhoods would once again thrive with lively interactions instead of people hunkered down in the safety of their homes.

What About Nature?

With all this fantastic futuristic stuff, the last thing we want is to destroy the pristine places created by the Cosmos, the Original World, or to tame them into some impersonal, modern fantasyland. We need raw Nature to be truly happy just like we need the stars at night and a clean sky with all its seasons and weather. These are messy organic things with bugs and animals and growth and decay. We need healthy oceans, lakes and streams teeming with life. Our mission is to find a balance between our needs and the needs of the other creatures of the planet. *We don't own the Earth.* This perfection is the key to both mental and spiritual wealth. When we are at balance with Nature, all is right.

So it will always be necessary to set aside large protected zones of:

Oceans and Seas	Wetlands
Forests	Lakes
Jungles	Rivers and streams
Deserts	Meadows
Mountains	Valleys and canyons
Plains	Parks
Plateaus and Mesas	Reserves

Some animals are so significant, they should have essentially their own nations. Africa is plenty large enough to set aside places where animals rule and live by ancient, original ways and not be forced to accommodate greedy humans. Humans should develop a non-interference directive for these zones.

In a state like New Jersey that left alone, wants to cover itself in thick forest, could create connected swaths of virgin forest where animals could live and travel freely according to their ways. Rather than trying to tame every bit of Nature we could learn to coexist knowing that we were doing the right thing by our fellow Earth inhabitants. We could still work to eradicate diseases in these areas such as rabies, distemper and various blights or invasive species, but always with the health of the ecological zone in mind.

Cities, likewise, should be filled with parks and gardens that celebrate Nature and glorify her beauty even incorporating safe passage channels connecting wilderness and animal migration. Without real estate moguls and greed controlling our every urban motivation, we would be free to find that perfect balance everywhere on Earth, greatly increasing our collective mental and spiritual wealth.

The Earth Has Rights

There are already countries such as Bolivia who have adopted a Bill of Rights for the Earth and Nature, affording the voiceless legal representation in the court system and protections under the Law. Organizations such as Earth Rights[17] and movements such as the Green Movement already fully recognize the need to vigorously protect the environment, animals and indigenous peoples from exploitation and ruination. By recognizing Earth and Animal Rights, we improve our standing in the Cosmos and we make peace with ourselves by remembering our roots and our One Mothership, the only one for light years around that gives us nearly Everything we have. In a world without money, the Earth only grows in importance as a living, breathing and majestic home for ourselves and our co inhabitants. On the other hand, to continue down the road we are on is to invite calamity and extinction. In the end the Earth can't stop to "care" about yet another one of millions of species that have come and gone over the eons. She's seen it all. The ball is in our court, not hers. We have absolutely no reason to have an adversarial relationship to our planet and every reason to have a loving, respectful one.

---

[17] https://earthrights.org

Extractive practices such as mining could be required to restore the site to its original purpose but that may be moot as more resources could be recycled and mined from asteroids. Farming practices would also change drastically with extensive use of hydroponics and organic, sustainable methods. The needs for torturing and killing sentient beings could be eliminated with delicious substitutes and eating could be a guilt-free activity.

The Golden Age of Medicine

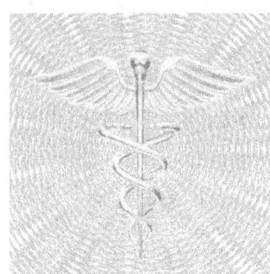

All physical maladies are curable. Whether by means of genetic fixes or eliminating microbial invaders in the body or reversing damage to organs, regenerating tissue, hearing, sight or other such marvels of medicine, this is where we are heading. Currently, immunotherapy is a growing field in which the "nanotechnology" of the body, our own immune systems are turned against cancer. Drexler theorizes that more advanced nanotechnology can repair bodies on a molecular level.

Of course, this brings up some of the hardest ethical quandaries known—what happens when we become if not immortal, beings of extreme longevity? Would we want to? What would we do with all that extra time? What prevents population explosion? Who decides who gets to have children? Would there be any children at all? If old people were young of body and mind would there be such a thing as elderly? Would marriage still be for life? So much of our culture is based on a normal lifespan of less than 100 years. Does hanging on to this physical life we know prevent us from moving on to another life? What if we died on this advanced world but then we were reincarnated into a more primitive world across the galaxy? In the end, we can't control our final fate, try as we may. Kurzweil thinks we can upload ourselves into machines, experiencing the same thoughts and feelings and sense of self. Who would protect us from being hacked and how would we know it was us and not the illusion of being ourselves with an entire new set of memories? This is perhaps life's greatest mystery—what makes us *us*?

Perhaps the ultimate freedom is to choose when to die. Dr. Philip Nitschke, a specialist in assisted suicide in Europe, has invented a somewhat creepy machine called Sarco[18] that ends life in a painless way at the time of one's choosing. It may be that after living 200 fantastic years on this planet, we might long for something beyond this material plane of existence or simply tire of it. We don't know because we've never had to worry about it.

On the other hand, we may decide to explore the Universe where *we* become the extraterrestrials and so an extremely long life may be required for traversing the vast expanses of the Cosmos. Nevertheless, how one would spend this time becomes an issue no matter where one was. Perhaps we would master suspended animation and could go dormant for long periods of time, awaking for periods of lively activity in interesting places. Perhaps this is already what happens to us when we die.

---

[18] https://exitinternational.net/sarco/

Work in the Future

Many of us like to work, some love to work and others hate to work, generally because they are forced to by society and doing something "functional" for someone else that doesn't excite them. In a way, it seems barbaric that a life could be spent as a tool or a cog in an imaginary profit machine for someone else. Nonetheless, many of us wrap our identity up in our jobs and it becomes who we are. I'm a teacher. I'm a doctor. I'm a plumber. No matter what you do during your day, your day will pass. You could sit perfectly still. You could run a triathlon. You could assemble cars. In the end, time has passed and gone forever all cases. What you do has no effect on time. *Time has an effect on you.*

No one has the answers for how life might turn out on Earth. It has great potential for both positive and negative outcomes, specifically with respect to human life. My personal prediction is based on what I've said above, that our relationship to, and need for, material wealth will become essentially obsolete. The days of cogs and human labor are numbered.

This is by no means to say there are not jobs in the future. We may decide and encode into our social contract that certain jobs are to never be automated, both as a safeguard and as a bastion of Humanity, to keep us ultimately in control of our own destiny.

This list of jobs would perhaps be controversial and difficult to arrive at for some would not agree and others may be convinced that an Artificial Entity could do a better job of it. For example what of these occupations:

Politicians and Representatives*
Boards of Directors
Spiritual Leaders (Priests, Imams, Monks, Rabbis, etc.)
Psychotherapists

Some jobs may be protected as desirable and us not willing to cede them to unfeeling robots or even those who appear to feel such as:

Artists	Counselors
Musicians	Mathematicians
Dancers	Theoretical scientists
Actors	Philosophers
Chefs	Astronomers
Park Rangers	Biologists
Naturalists	Archeologists
Anthropologists	Historians
Socratic Tutors	Any "ology
Administrators	

Some of these will most assuredly have automated counterparts but there may always be an appetite for a fellow human to be doing certain things at certain times, if not only for nostalgia.

Other jobs can be easily seen to be endangered and we have a very long history of jobs becoming obsolete. These include:

Drivers of all sorts
Pilots and train engineers
Astronauts
Factory workers
Lawyers
Some types of Doctors, even surgeons[19]
Some types of Nurses
Accountants
Programmers

Basically any job that could be done as well or better by a skilled robot or Artificially Intelligent Entity. Any job that was tedious, repetitive or dangerous would be replaced by efficient automation that required no salary, no benefits and had no concept of "working a shift." In other cases, jobs that required precision and extraordinary knowledge and vision could be automated beyond human skill and sensory levels since in automation mathematical precision is the standard. So surgery in hard to reach places could be far less intrusive by employing miniature devices that could find their way, excise and remove or repair tissue.

However, in many of these cases, replacement may not even be desired and we may want a more assistive approach where the robots and AI agents are helpful tools to enhance the practitioner's skill, dexterity or knowledge. We already have such a system in place with knowledge at our fingertips and all manner of wizardly machinery to assist us so this would continue to gain in power one way or another.

We could see, at least at first, a class of jobs dedicated to "babysitting" and maintaining these automated workers. Later, as time progressed, these jobs would also become superfluous because they too could be largely automated or even unneeded. Regardless, the number of minders needed would be exponentially fewer than the number of people currently employed. For example, you can already visit and automated Amazon distribution center and see only a handful of humans overseeing a busy swarm of robots fetching, packaging and filing away millions of items 24-7. This clear trend can be seen at other automated plants as well.

*Politicians may in fact be replaced, or at least aided by, superior artificial intelligent agents that can utilize a vast resource of historical data, facts and inputs and quickly and efficiently make policy decisions that will benefit the most people while not violating the rights of individuals. Even a position as high as the Presidency could be usurped by such an Agent due to its ability to understand and digest far more information than a human can. A human could be a signatory to such decisions as a final check.

Sustainability and The Economy of Enough

Even in a magical world that freely creates and distributes Cosmic Products, we have to have an

---

[19] https://blogs.scientificamerican.com/observations/the-surgical-singularity-is-approaching/

understanding of what is Enough[20]. We can't become next-level consumers just because we don't have to pay. We can still want or have too much. Much more than we need. Robots could efficiently clear the oceans of fish, the forests of trees. We have to have a Relationship with the Earth and care deeply about her condition and needs so we can operate within the Zone of Sustainability. Sustainability is a pretty easy test to check for. Does an action degrade the ecosphere over a longer period? If it does, it's not sustainable. Does the action deplete a Practical Resource at a rate that it will be used up for future generations? When we live only for ourselves and not for future generations too, we are pigs at the trough to be despised by the people of the Future. However, if we operate with Love and Good Will toward ourselves, the Earth and those Future People and Animals, we will operate sustainably. Put more simply, the meek (the sustainable) shall inherit the Earth.

You can't address sustainability without addressing population. At the present world population growth rate of 1.1% per year it will take about 63 years to double the world's population. Since we are already using/wasting more resources than the Earth can replenish, this is a serious problem. Basically, some assets of Physical Wealth are already in a negative or debt scenario. Overcrowding and congestion in cities is already a major problem, not to mention all the pollution and garbage that is generated. This is not sustainable without major changes in behavior. In order to bring this under control we would have to manage our birthrates and how we use resources fairly drastically. Otherwise, a primary foundation of Physical Wealth, the Ecosphere will fall into poverty and debt. Such a debt, if allowed to grow like we do with imaginary financial debt would lead to calamity. With financial debt you can simply declare bankruptcy and move on. With Physical Debt, bankruptcy can lead directly to death, even of entire species. Extinction is a form of biological bankruptcy, from which there is no recovery.

To avoid this we will have to do the following:

Eliminate all business and enterprise that chronically degrades the environment
Stop wasting food
Stop using plastic by making new biodegradable materials
Stop introducing toxins to water and ground and improve water purification techniques
Reduce birth rates until they roughly match death rates
Determine the optimal population on Earth, not including space residents
Wean off of fossil fuels to electromagnetic systems driven by renewable
Stop deforestation and replant crucial forests
Green up cities including use of hydroponic local farming
Embrace sustainable farming practices, reducing chemical dependency. This can also be helped greatly with robots that can zap bugs instead of using pesticides. Hydroponics are easier to manage in this regard but may not be practical for large grain crops
Reduce meat and fish intake
Reduce average domicile footprint
Reduce paved areas, replace with solar roads

---

[20] The term "Economy of Enough" was coined from mathematician and entrepreneur, Dr. Carl Ledbetter

None of this needs to negatively impact the quality of life. As shown above we could enjoy unprecedented levels of all forms of wealth. It's more a matter of adjusting our expectations to live within the Earth's means but to do it with flair, artistry and without excessive wants in a more Mindful existence.

Population control becomes even more of a challenge when longevity rises and medical breakthroughs promise to only increase this, reducing the death rate. Therefor we have to make sure not to have a corresponding rise in birth rates or the Earth will be overrun by a "human infestation" more than it already is.

Michael Ben-Eli has written extensively on this topic as have many others and I would recommend you read his treatise, *Sustainability: The Five Core Principles*[21].

All the Lonely People

Socrates famously said, "The unexamined life is not worth living." We live in an epidemic of unexamined lives right now. And I don't only mean examining our own lives, either. So much time is spent on externalities of work, purchasing and constant entertainment, or I should say stimulation, that very few of us stop to smell the roses or to ponder the meaning of it all, let alone the plight of a neighbor suffering from loneliness two houses down. This shallowness affects every part of life and produces in us loneliness, emptiness, anxiety and depression, all on the rise in the 2010's.

This means we are doing something wrong. If loneliness, anxiety and depression are on the rise, then something must be done to reverse this trend because that is not a healthy status for humanity and will only lead to an evermore dysfunctional society.

Plato, in his Allegory of the Cave[22] likened much of life to living in the darkness of a cave, developing a view of the world based on shadows and lights not truly understanding the causes of the shadows and lights. Only through concerted effort can someone possibly escape the cave into the light of day and gain a deeper understanding. But that's not enough, those that escape have an innate duty to return to the cave and help others escape. That becomes a great purpose in life. Loneliness is also a type of cave but in a way worse than Plato's cave because there are no companions to share the shadows with. Anything one can do to provide love and companionship to the lonely and the forgotten will surely create a richer, more rewarding life than one spent pursuing only self-satisfaction. Not only will this fill a void for the one we give companionship and dialog, but it will also fill a void in us, a double bonus!

Our Biggest Expense: Spending Time

When one *spends* time, one spends the most valuable asset, by far, and one that grows infinitely more valuable as it passes by. Therefore time has the highest cost when spent. Time is also the

---

[21] https://www.bfi.org/sites/default/files/attachments/pages/Sustainability-FiveCorePrinciples-BenEli.pdf

[22] https://en.wikipedia.org/wiki/Allegory_of_the_Cave

most easily wasted commodity because it always passes no matter what we do.

Our mastery of genetics and ecological issues would leave us in a much better condition than we see today.

The remaining areas of mastery would be mental and spiritual in nature. This is what our time would go toward. By changing our needs structure, we will also change our time usage, putting it back in control of the individual and greatly increasing freedom for all.

With no need to work for a living people could spend their time pursuing anything they wanted, not limited to but including:

Learning	Boating	Knitting, weaving and
Practicing	Athletics	crochet
Crafts	Discussion	Sports
Arts	Traveling	Debate
Reading	Space travel	Virtual reality
Gaming	Social duties	Tripping
Gardening	Cleaning both home	Farming
Raising children	and environment	Sightseeing
Teaching	Bird watching	Whale watching
Meditating	Collecting	Scuba diving
Hiking	Museums	Submarines
Ceremonies	Entertainment	Astronomy
Gift giving	Concerts	Languages
Puzzles	Composing	Mathematics
Comedy	Archery	Poetry
Antiquing	Sex	Writing
Trading	Yoga	Movie making
Skydiving	Tutoring	Dancing
Flying	Coaching	Cooking
Training	Planting	Storytelling
Maintenance	Jewelry making	Writing
Governing	Mediation	Magic
Judging	Astronomy	Training
Law making	Exercize	Worship/Rituals
Biking	Model building	Being

These many rewarding activities are to be joined by many more and will be adequate for us to add meaning and purpose to our lives outside the tedium of working for a living. We will simply live to live, *free of drudgery and exploitation.*

The Powerlessness of Politics and Isms to Stop Real Progress

Regardless of one's political beliefs, the physical world will continue to change, evolve and operate according to the laws of physics. One could vote for ONLY coal and oil for decades and because of physics, the Earth and Sun would terminate the conditions supporting life. One could be super angry with "liberals" and want to punish them by following a self-destructive agenda and the Earth and Sun would not care or change anything they do in the slightest and one would also be punished. One could create large, refrigerated underground cities to house like-minded people but eventually one would encounter the same problems, only in a less desirable place. The relationships between Money, Value and Cosmic Resources would not change. In the "safe" underground city, there still could be haves and have-nots, owners and renters, management and labor or it could all be automated as it was above ground and then one may have "the robot owners" and everybody else sort of like *Westworld*[23]. The question will always be what power the "everybody else" is allowed to have.

Another dystopian possibility is even more likely though the probability is impossible for me to estimate, that of devolution or even extinction. We have so many threats to life from asteroids, infection, nukes to runaway experiments, nanobot invasions or even Terminator-like AI but one is looming bigger than all of these: Climate Change. Given the right set of circumstances, the Earth could create a feedback mechanism called an Attractor in Chaos Theory and go into hothouse conditions, squelching Life as we know it. Money could not buy its way out of this because it would be happening on a scale far greater than money touches, the Solar Realm. The Sun, a star, is not for sale, can't be bought off and can't be altered by money. Money can buy sunblock or an umbrella but it can't change the 275 trillion horsepower of solar energy hitting the Earth 24-7-365.

Ray Kurzweil, an inventor and futurist, wrote a book called the *The Singularity is Near*. In it he describes a soon approaching time when Artificial Intelligence is allowed to improve itself at a geometric rate, far surpassing our biological intelligence and the abilities of the human brain. Now he goes much further and posits that such AI will in fact become conscious and whatsmore we will be able to download our own minds into hardware and essentially become immortal, space-ready travelers of the Cosmos. I find that to be a bit presumptuous since we still haven't solved the mystery of consciousness and self-awareness but I do think the AI will enable all of the things regarding solving world problems in poverty of all types.

And such things will happen regardless of political systems, ideology or beliefs because in science, one thing leads to another. In order to stop this from happening you'd need to have a catastrophe of some sort to stop progress in its tracks and reset the clock. Eventually, even such setbacks would be overcome and the same circumstances would arise.

Power: Who Will Have It?

Does all this mean the power structures of society will greatly change and if so, who or what will actually be in control of the Laws, the Policies, the Access to these endless material overflows?

---

[23] https://en.wikipedia.org/wiki/Westworld_(TV_series)

Will we be allowed to simply live in peace or will there be those who will seek to control the mechanisms, the flows and amounts of material goods. If left unregulated, we could see a new type of hoarder, who would freely accumulate some thing or things that could overflow physical space of neighbors, piling up all around, possibly endangering others. Who would police this? What is the role of the criminal in such a society? It is possible new types of crimes would emerge where the mechanisms of delivery could be impeded or teaching robots could be programmed to brainwash people into apathy or to perform some nefarious sabotage to a competing system and otherwise wrest control away for their own purposes.

Governments would be expected to regulate all of this and unless the government too was automated with AI geniuses making wise decisions, there would be Human Officials in control of these regulatory bodies. If automated, who would oversee these complex systems beyond human understanding, created by generations of hyper-intelligent agents we would much less understand than we currently understand the inner working of an iPhone.

The most fraught period would be the transition where those currently in power would need to be convinced of the illusory nature of the power they have. Some would be very reluctant to give up an advantage they enjoy. However, over time, they would see those advantages erode as more and more people were of equal material status. There is potential for violent confrontation in protection of the status quo but one would need to ask to what end? What is the real purpose of power if not to secure material advantage and wealth? By taking away this reason, then we would be left with those who enjoy power for power's sake, the ability to lord it over others. One presumes that the numbers of such people would not be significant and that they would eventually capitulate to a superior model of society where they too could enjoy all the same benefits.

Dystopia: The Other Possibilities and Green Meat

A positive outcome may be consciously manipulated to happen for only a privileged few, maintaining the status quo of History. Those in power today may continue to control all the main levers of policy, progress and technology in such a way as to dictate the availability of Cosmic Products to certain classes of people only and the amounts and quality thereof. If we used the same proportions of wealthy to non-wealthy that exists today, less than 5% of people would be Masters and the other 95% would be powerless against the robots and AI used to protect the Masters and their power. Such a system would be difficult to overcome and these differences would only grow as time went by, further locking the masses out from the Cosmic Bounty.

There are copious models for dystopian societies and science fiction abounds with these:

The Time Machine: Where a pacified distant future population has forgotten all it learned and mindlessly heed the siren to report for dinner, as food for the underground, albino Morlocks.

Wall-i: Where we become fat slobs in lounge chairs on cosmic cruise ships nursing on the teet of Virtual Reality

The Matrix: Where we become "batteries" for the machine overlords who keep us satiated and plugged into a virtual world by directly jacking into our brains

Terminator: Where AI and robots become our mortal enemies seeking to annihilate us as so much biological detritus

Soylent Green: Where overpopulation forces people to report to self termination centers to be euthanized (very nicely I might add) and then processed into food substance for the masses (not the elites)

Logan's Run: Where we are embedded at birth with a sort of timer and when we hit that certain age and the timer goes off we are terminated (another population control method)

1984: Where "Big Brother" is watching everything you do and controlling every aspect of society

AI: Where machines mimic consciousness and human emotion so well that we find ourselves in an ethical conundrum regarding how we treat them, similar to *Westworld's* premise.

In each of these tales there are serious ethical and philosophical issues raised about what we want to become, the kind of world we are making *right now* and the decisions we are making that will impact future generations.

The Future of Art and Music

When drum machines came along, drummers were told their days were numbered and in many instances this was somewhat true. It was more expensive to hire a drummer for a recording, set up elaborate microphones for each drum and rehearse the takes. Economics made for some lesser musical quality produced by a machine with perfect timing yet lacking in organic human feel. Drum machines have improved greatly since then yet drummers are still in demand by other musicians and audiences. It turns out we like the human aspect of music, no matter how good the artificial music is. Also, it turned out that drummers know how to program drum machines best because of their innate knowledge of drumming and how to best emphasize beats.

Likewise when you follow the history of instruments from their acoustic roots into the age of synthesizers, brought about by the telephone company trying to improve transmissions and clarity, you find similar threats to the practicing musician, be it an oboe player on Broadway or a string section in a jingle recording. Synthesizers have now become not only great imitators of classic instruments, but have pushed well beyond into a new sonic frontier often combining classic sounds with synthetic ones or by applying new "envelopes" to the sound giving composers and musicians endless new possibilities.[24]

---

[24] http://www.holistictonality.org

Now with AI, even the composer is threatened. There are companies that specialize in generated music compositions where you enter the mood, the tempo and a few other parameters and presto, the music is composed for you. I even created a program in the 1990's called *Presto* to do exactly that. As I mentioned above, my Art Fountain software does the same thing with visual arts—using algorithms, but not AI, removing the artist from the physical process of drawing and painting. Yet people still want real paintings and real music that come out of the hands of people and this may never change.

That said, I firmly believe that as artists we will always be in a collaboration with technology, no matter how advanced it gets and that as instruments and art creation methods and media change we will be able to produce new music and new art that was hitherto impossible to create. Each generation deserves a chance to push the boundaries and to find new ways to express themselves, building on the work of the past.

In the end, it will be us sentient beings that decide if art or music is good and not an audience of robots but just because it was made using an automated process doesn't mean we won't like it. We will, but no one will go to see a concert where someone presses a button one time and music is created. They'll have to at least hit the button three times for us to be impressed!

Through AI, light projection, advanced displays, virtual reality and myriad algorithms we will be able to have art in more places to inspire us in many new ways but we will always be more impressed and more inspired when truly skilled and inspired artists are behind the creation and meaning of the art.

When imagination is fully exhausted, only then will art die.

The Bridge to the Cosmic Age: The Assistive Period

Entering the Cosmic Age will not happen overnight and could take hundreds of years. Nevertheless, so many of the pieces of what we can do are already possible and can start to alleviate the suffering of humanity and Nature starting today, even keeping our current monetary mechanisms in place. We already are experiencing some of the benefits of automation in the form of lower costs for many goods and services. With proper focus and wise policy making, these trends can be accelerated to achieve big things right this minute including:

    Robots to clean the ocean and manage landfills and recycling
    Robots to build affordable electric vehicles
    Much lower prices on all manner of goods
    Improved healthcare services and lower pharmaceutical costs
    Better time management with AI used in scheduling of trains and planes
    Lower costs for basic legal, accounting and medical services
    Assistive devices for workers, households and the elderly
    Improved fire protection and security
    Automated vehicles of all sorts including: cars, trucks, trains, planes and ships
    Shorter work weeks and days

If done with compassion and care, these things can drastically lower the cost of living and reduce poverty, clean the environment, shrink the work week and free up billions of man-years of wasted time to enable the efforts required to enter the Cosmic Age.

Many of the advances in society are not directly correlated to automation or even computing and these should continue unabated such as: advances in philosophy, ethics, science and mathematics, the arts and literature, entertainment. This includes cures for diseases, new materials and too many things to list but all of these can add to the quality of life and diminish suffering. Some advances can have the opposite effect such as what we've seen with plastic—a seemingly amazing new material (back then) with a nasty side effect of never fully leaving the ecosphere.

Because there will be much less inequity, many of the social consequences will fade during this period and things like social bullying, teasing, cliques and even acne of other thing teens suffer from today will become a relic of a more primitive time. The level of education will rise also, producing more informed citizens, leading to wiser governance.

Properly implemented, Assistive Automation should *always* produce downward pressure on cost and a lowering of prices. Complete Automation of the production chain reduces cost to near zero and those costs can be paid without money. No system except for the Universe itself can have absolute zero cost.

The Diminishing Influence of Money

As the Cosmic Age approaches money will rapidly become less interesting and useful to most people. Certain careers in money-making will dwindle such as all things related to trading and investing. There will be no need to invest or to even save money because of its worthlessness to the folks of the future. Banks and insurance companies will disappear just like the coal railroads and the printing press did before. The cashless society is on the road to a moneyless society because it completely *virtualizes* the monetary transaction. When all money exists as 1's and 0's in the cloud it naturally leads to the full realization of the intangible nature money has had all along and so the transfer of digital money eventually becomes absurd.

Prolonging the Assistive Age

It could turn out that powers that be will not allow or society at large is not able to make the leap to a world where we are fully responsible for our own mental well-being, our time, and prefer to be coddled by a corporate or state-run nanny system, finding purpose in doing jobs and spending time on others' work schedules. In this case the Assistive Age could be thought of as a New and Improved Automated Industrial Age and the paradigms of work for pay and pay for goods could be perpetuated, hopefully in a more equitable manner. Otherwise, we will merely be delaying the inevitable for the wrong reasons and running the risk of unsustainability and social inequality based on a sort of social lottery based on birth rights and generational wealth.

Resisting the Assistive Age

Because we are bridging to a job-threatening then job-ending phase from a job-needing phase many people will see automated processes, especially those in public places, as a threat to personal freedom and security. This is a dicey situation because it will prompt violent behavior toward the automatons which in turn will prompt greater security measures from the owners thereof. If left to escalate, it could set up a negative dynamic between people and their would be eventual liberators. In fact the number of attacks on self-driving vehicles is increasing and they haven't even started taking over jobs in earnest. Sabotage can be expected to reach a peak level some time early in the Assistive Age and will be best dealt with by assuring guaranteed income and as quickly as possible frame the automation as a benefit to all and not a privilege to the few.

Artificial Flaws and Pitfalls

Artificial Intelligence and Machine Learning have many nefarious uses for malfeasance. With the advent of "Deep Fake" video and audio production, indistinguishable fakes can be used as evidence, news and be presented as true, making it harder for society to progress and reach accord on policy. Disinformation is perhaps the most dangerous of all weapons because it can create mass hysteria, embolden large groups to act irrationally, create false conspiracies and cause endless legal machinations, wasting time getting to the real facts. Even worse, it can cause people to lose faith in facts themselves undermining a cornerstone of democracy—educated masses making informed decisions. This then opens the doors for autocrats and manipulators to hijack government and maintain power, preventing progress.

Chapter 4: gOS—The Government Operating System

One can consider the Constitution and our body of Laws to be an operating system of sorts. We can call this gOS 1.0. At this point it's a patchwork of antiquated bug fixes where we've had to correct earlier mistakes such as with regard to Slavery and Women's Rights. Also, many parts are vaguely worded, leading to endless disputes, arguments and cases before the Supreme Court. Honestly, like all software eventually does, it needs a rewrite from scratch.

The reasons to include this section are many but most importantly, there is a necessity for extreme safety, coordination and efficiency to even begin to implement an automated system of the magnitude contemplated here. Driverless vehicles and planes transporting materials, people and products alone requires software systems that connect to traffic controls, sensors and the like. Sending robots out to clean oceans, perform farming in a timely manner, fight fires and remove waste can't be coordinated by disparate systems that don't communicate. On top of all of these reasons, there is a need to improve and protect the pillars of Democracy and to extend it further into the Animal Kingdom and the Earth itself to create a sustainable, holistic system. Then, there are the advantages yet to be taken of new technologies to improve how we vote, how decisions are made and who can be elected to represent us at every level of society. Finally, I'm a software developer by trade and so I have a clear vision on what software does, how it it made and when it is needed. So make no mistake, while we will be greatly assisted by automation, we should never be blindly led by it nor cede ultimate decision-making to non-sentient beings.

It would be most wise as a species, or at least as a nation to start creating a gOS 2.0, a software that works very much like any *Objective Programming* language, such as a modern day Operating System we see on our devices (eg. Windows or Mac OS or Linux). I have in another document started sketching out what a system would look like but in a nutshell it would be a *vast* system of Frameworks built on a Core Foundation. At the heart of the Foundation would be a system of *immutable* morals and principles regarding human, animal and Earth rights. All higher frameworks would inherit the properties of all of the more fundamental and foundational frameworks. For example, one might have an *Object* called a Department. The Department would inherit from Frameworks for Oversight which would inherit from Rules which would inherit from Something else and so on until it got to the Core Foundation. This way, each Department would share certain properties and attributes and behaviors that were common to all departments.

We would need something akin to a Department of Commerce but because selling things would be obsolete it would likely morph into a Department of Distribution, governing the equitable and healthy sharing of the Cosmic Products. Scientifically and humanely Coordinating Information and Material Distribution to nodes in the system where they benefit the most people and animals would have a huge benefit to life.

Like any software, one would expect gOS to be continually upgraded and improved and its conceivable that certain versions could become buggy or broken or even hacked by bad actors, human or otherwise.

By having a brilliant gOS, society could govern itself beautifully and efficiently and decisions could be made based on scientific needs measured against moral principles. Such a government would operate beyond the primitive domain of parties, tribalism and politics.

In such a system data would be highly integrated, measuring everything from the weather, the motion of vehicles and electrical usages, etc. This would allow for much more up-to-date and better preventive and reactive measures in the cases of storms and other types of disasters.

The main purpose of gOS is to protect and serve the people and the animals of the nation and the world.

gOS would involve extensive use of AI for politically-neutral assistive decision making on Global, National, State and Local levels. People would interact with gOS based on role and security clearance.

gOS would make extensive use of Artificial Intelligence, Machine Learning, Neural Networks, Blockchain, Databases, Algorithms, Quantum Computing and Communications.

Core G: The Immutable Principles

What is the Job of Government?

To secure the most benefits for the most people and creatures (Animal Rights Framework) for the longest time. These benefits are based on Six guiding *immutable* principles:

Essential Environment: Air, Water and Land Purity and Stewardship.

Essential Rights: Human, Personal, Animal and Earth

Essential Wisdom: Sustainability, Knowledge, Common Sense, Science, Mathematics, Compassion, History, Accountability

Essential Safety: Medical, Police, Fire, Military, etc.

Essential Beauty: Aesthetics, Architecture, Signage and the Arts

Essential Trust: Verification, Truth, Certification, Standards, Privacy

When all six of these principles have been fully respected, it is possible to live a healthy, happy life the way it was meant to be. When any are compromised, we experience strife and life becomes difficult or more unpleasant. These principles are not subject to change for they are to represent Universally accepted norms of operating a clean and moral society that proudly leaves to the next generation the same or a better world, but never worse. Therefore they are said to be immutable.

We may find that certain conflicts arise such as between policing and privacy. By proper use of the Judicial Framework, most of these conflicts can be resolved and by protecting privacy using encrypted blockchains, we can assure that only those with proper access rights can gain entry to private data and only the specific data needed.

These are going to be the Core Objects of our gOS. All Frameworks will inherit from these core objects so that in order for a policy to be certified by gOS it must satisfy the six Core objects. The beauty of an Operating System is it's never complete and is constantly being improved, tweaked and added to as life changes. This is one of the innate qualities of gOS: Mutability. We are not interested in any system for the system's sake. We want results so any changes that give us better results that don't violate the Core are welcome.

There is no concept of Party in gOS. Party is an obsolete concept that causes unnecessary divisions in society that have nothing to do with practical goals that are shared by all. In fact, as you will see in the Electoral Framework, party politics is not allowed.

We already have the fragments of gOS. Every government on Earth now requires software and huge computer systems to operate. There is no other way to coordinate and keep records and connect departments to one another. These vast databases and networks however operate largely in siloed and disconnected ways that often increase chaos and bureaucracy. Only by reinventing all of it from the ground up, from scratch, could we create a real gOS where every bit of data and each department shared common resources to optimize decision making, distribution of goods and services and protection of life.

It would be impossible to govern a large system such as a Dyson Sphere or even the Earth itself (not a nation within) without a gOS. So many processes would need to be automated beyond the comprehension and ability of the biological mind and the operation thereof would require great coordination of resources and split-second decision making on a massive scale that voting and traditional bureaucracy would fail miserably.

Beauty is subjective and as they say, in the eye of the beholder. However, when we look around in Nature we find a common starting point of pleasing palettes and shapes that are part of our evolutionary heritage. If we use Nature as a guide, we can find agreeable design principles that satisfy the most people. We can all agree that hanging wires and cables everywhere and placing too many billboards or clashing signs is not beautiful. In the Cosmic Age, advertising would be far less desperate for our attention and much of it would disappear. Many towns already have strict guidelines on architecture and signage and often these places are the most desirable locations because of it. The first principle is to care about aesthetics.

Harmonious color palettes taken from the Grand Canyon and the sky

The Foundational Frameworks

These are the FrameWorks that represent the core organs of governance and each of these are parents to many other sub FrameWorks that inherit the properties of the parent, topmost being the Core framework:

Core Framework: This is the *Principle Framework* that ALL others inherit from based on the the Six Immutable Principles above.

Foundation Framework: This is the *Practical Framework* that operates government based on the Core Principles of Democracy and the very purpose of a nation's existence. Within this framework the sacred principles and the Bill of Rights 2.0, updated for the modern age, become action in the world.

Electoral framework: Governs the way we campaign for offices and how we mechanically go about electing officials in a standardized, fair manner.

Federal Elections Framework

State Election Framework

Local Election Framework

Executive Framework: Governs the behavior of top-level decision making and the enforcement of laws

Urban Management Framework: Governs how cities are to be built and run

Rural Management Framework: Governs how rural areas are used and developed

Law Enforcement framework: Governs policing

Military Framework: Governs the use and deployments of armed forces

Diplomatic Framework: Governs the bodies that represent us in foreign lands

Safety Framework: Governs how emergency services or run

Legislative Framework: Governs how laws are written, changed and deprecated

Representative Framework: Governs the rules of the House of Representatives 2.0

Senate Framework: *Deprecated*

Elected Expert Framework: Essentially, this sub-branch of the Legislative Branch supplants the now-obsolete Senate which has become overly political and undemocratic. Instead, area-specific *Boards of Experts* will be convened and chosen through the Electoral Framework. While the House Representatives are peer-based citizens from the general population, these decision makers will be knowledgeable on the topics on which they are making decisions.

Judicial Framework: Governs how Laws are interpreted and the Cause of Justice is served

Legal Framework: Governs the actions of lawyers

Bench Framework: Governs the actions of judges

Cosmic Framework: Governs the creation and distribution of Cosmic Products and the creation thereof

> **Cosmic Resource Management Framework:** Governs the extraction and handling of raw resources provided by the Cosmos

> **Cosmic Production Framework:** Governs the conversion of Cosmic Resources into useful products

> **Distribution Framework:** Governs the equitable and healthy distribution of Cosmic Products to the Nation(s)

One Highlighted Framework

It's not really the scope of this book to delve into the gOS as that would be a highly technical and vast endeavor capable of filling perhaps millions of pages to be complete. All one need to to see this is search online regarding the structure and departments of the US or Chinese governments to see the depth of bureaucracy either required or required to replace with something better.

Even detailing the inner workings of one of these frameworks would be a daunting task and would require years of research to do properly so below I will merely sketch out and example in rough detail for the **Electoral Framework** and will in no way be complete. The reader may find things they think could be added or subtracted.

Each framework has a set of properties. Think these as numbers and words and other data types like images, movies, time stamps, etc. The framework itself simply operates on these properties with a set of algorithms and methods and returns "an answer" to a problem posed or question asked. The framework is a problem solver and an answer giver, relying entirely on the data provided to the framework and the integrity of other frameworks that are "called" from within this framework. The integrity of a framework is determined by conformance to established standards. Most of the time, the reply from the framework will be an **Object** with the properties filled in as expected, not a simple number or text, though certain methods of the Framework would return simple data.

Example Properties and Methods of an Electoral Framework might include and also be common to other frameworks:

Framework ID: The main identifier for the framework

Framework Change History: An accessor to the full history of changes made to the Framework tying into the Auditing Framework

Last Modified: Timestamp for the last time the Framework was modified tying into the Auditing Framework

Mission statement: The stated purpose of the framework pulled from the Mission Framework using the ID

Population Data: Pulled from the Demographics Framework

Eligible Voter Data: An object pulled from the Voter Registration Framework, including Voter ID's

Vote Count: Object Pulled from the Voting Framework based on Entity Type and Entity ID. For example local voting tallies for Maplewood, NJ or State results for Idaho.

Winner: Another object pulled from the Voting Framework based on Entity Type and Entity ID and Role ID, the position voted for.

Candidates: An object listing eligible candidates, their profiles and background information and districts

Districts: Data on distinct voting districts including the Method used to draw the district lines and a list of officials overseeing the voting process in the district

Voting Method: An object detailing the accepted secure voting methods

Counting Method: An object detailing the accepted methods of vote counting and verification

Blockchain Accessors: Providing access to protected private Voter data used for secure electronic voting

Voting Status: Object returning the voting status (whether a person voted) based on Voter ID

Election Timelines: Object returning the dates for registration, early voting and election day deadlines

Election Errors: Access to data provided by the Election Auditing Framework

Framework Planning: Access to the Roadmap for improvements and objectives slated for the Electoral Framework

Protection of the gOS Source Code

As we know from mathematics and computer science, no logical system is complete and always must rely on something outside of itself to operate. This is a fact of Reality. Theoretically, the gOS could be hacked or otherwise tampered with by malevolent actors. If done on a core level, then such changes could propagate to all levels outward relying on those Frameworks, very much like a bug in any modern operating systems can cause major problems. Therefore, extra special precautions would be taken to protect the Core Frameworks which would have highly restricted access, be highly encrypted and include a blockchain chronicling every minute change that was made so it could be verified at any time.

Democratic Society would be responsible for making sure sufficient numbers of skilled people were trained in the management and care of these nearly sacred parts of our Foundational Assistance Systems. Otherwise, in a certain way, society would deserve the consequences of becoming apathetic and unskilled and would experience major setbacks or even possible annihilation buy a global rogue system run amok. We may find the best way to store this code is just has Nature has found, in enormous strands of helical molecules, i.e. DNA with copies distributed billions of times a la blockchain.

The Differences Between Nations

Just because one nation forges ahead in areas of automation, extended intelligence and operating systems doesn't mean all nations will. Therefore we can expect a period where all sorts of bizarre imbalances could take place. While Cosmic Resources themselves obey no such artificial lines drawn between nations and in fact belong to all people of Earth (the Cosmos) equally, those in power and the societies themselves may be bent on title and claim to Cosmic Resources found within their borders. This is natural and may take centuries to get over as a meaningless and unhelpful division. Those nations that forge ahead could form a pact to freely share within the pact and even offer the same to those outside the pact so that over time, the old divisions would eventually fade into History.

There can also be cultural differences that make it difficult to accept equality and an end to disparity. For example, in a caste system, based on religious beliefs, the higher castes may resist the notion of lower castes being elevated materially. In other cases, remote tribes who have never evolved a materialistic culture would either not be interested in participating in some far-fetched futuristic world or us outsiders may decide that they belong on the Nature side of the equation and would work to preserve these indigenous cultures as they are.

COS: The Cosmic Operating System

Of course all of this may be old hat. If the cosmologists who believe we are living in a simulation already are right, then any system we create will already be running in a higher order operating system and our gOS would simply be a small subroutine in that system that is running flawlessly, upholding the laws of physics and math.

However, if no such system exists, gOS could expand to a Galactic Level and then go Intergalactic, coordinating quadrillions of worlds in a large Cosmic Network. Or there could be one heading our way already from another far more advanced world.

Chapter 5: The Cosmic Age

All of these things, happening as hitherto described, would usher in what can be referred to as the Cosmic Age, what some might also call the Golden Age. The Cosmic Age will begin when:

Automated systems subsume all manufacturing, extraction and distribution
Materialism is no longer prevalent
Hunger and poverty are eliminated
Money is obsolete as are all attendant mechanisms
Cosmic Products are freely distributed
The Earth is clean with large wilderness areas
Mental and Spiritual Wealth reign supreme

Various parts described in this chapter have already happened to one degree or another and are thus already proven as possible. The Cosmic Age merely means that they will be commonplace and not so extraordinary. Certain things below will happen much faster than others as parts of the already unfolding Information Age, an extension of the Enlightenment and Industrial Revolution. But until they are free to all and poverty is abolished, they will remain in the control of commercial interests.

People of the Future

The first thing one would notice not too far into the Cosmic Age is the people would be much healthier, a bit smarter on average and would probably make an unwitting time traveller from the past feel inferior and inadequate. It's hard to say how big they will be, what their hair will looks like, or not, and other such details but they will have more control over these things so they may tend to be taller and generally better looking. More importantly, they will have a different attitude and purpose in life and will not be nearly as concerned with the "rat race" issues we suffer from today. One supposes there will still be a competitive nature and so there can be expected to always be those that stand out in various fields of endeavor. Leadership will still be a quality that is looked to in decision-makers who help maintain the social structure, whether on a local level or higher.

If Space becomes more commonly inhabited and births start taking place then we might even see an evolutionary track of people who are more adapted to space living, perhaps even losing the ability to operate easily in the higher gravity environment of the Earth.

Paradise: The Age-old Mission

We have told ourselves the story of paradise in every culture. Paradise will certainly mean different things to different people. For understandable reasons, paradise is always beyond our reach and something we aspire to and even die for in some cases. No one says we can only have one paradise. We have achieved mini-paradise moments in History and as individuals where everything seems just right. By insisting on this as our persistent model rather than a fleeting moment we could enter a Golden Age of personal fulfillment, beauty and true happiness. We tend to settle for much less or give up when it seems unattainable but with a little extra help and focus we can finally reach what was once impossible to imagine on Earth and claim what the Cosmos has provided for us all along.

However, it is dangerous and somewhat cowardly to settle for our version of Paradise when out there may be waiting a far greater one. If God exists for example, there could be a state of being that far transcends everything we could possibly experience in a physical world. One can imagine a state of bliss without time where one becomes pure Love or experiences emotions we haven't felt with an intensity that is unimaginable. For all we know, stars are living spirits radiating out that pure energy from the Cosmic Source and we could eventually graduate to be such a being ourselves.

Utopia vs. Paradise

Other forms of Paradise exist also. Worlds of exquisite beauty and perfection where fragrances are sublime, gardens of fantastic flowers and majestic trees, gemlike structures abound and life on a higher plane of existence are possible. If it can be imagined, then it may actually exist. In many ways, the Earth is already such a place, a beautiful blue oasis with beautiful fragrant flowers and trees, majestic oceans and mountains, etc. All that is missing is a higher form of life to appreciate it all. So the real quest for Paradise may be, and has always been an inward quest to perfect ourselves and to become worthy of the life we have been given. Perhaps Adam and Eve did in fact live in Paradise right here on Earth.

We may want to divide these paradisiacal potentials into two forms:

Utopia: Where the imagined trappings of paradise are constructed in the material world and is achievable on the material plane of existence.

Paradise: Where things are less imaginable and exist on a higher plane of existence where for example there could be many more colors than we see and emotional depth far greater than we can contain physically.

Architecture

Goethe, the German writer and thinker, called architecture "frozen music." Architecture plays a huge role in our lives both in what we see around us and the places we live in. So much of what we've built was always limited in what we could afford to do within a given budget. In the Cosmic Age, no such limits would exist and we would mostly be limited by space and imagination. Buildings of unimaginable "musical" richness could be essentially printed from ingenious blueprints, making what used to be only available to kings and the wealthy commonplace. The world would transform before us into a magical place. The benefits are so many but most importantly, the blight of poverty would be finally defeated and there would no longer be the concept of a slum or a ghetto. Mental Health would improve as people would be surrounded by beauty creating a higher plane of consciousness.

There is no reason for any architecture to be permanent and in permanence is a sort of unfairness to those who may have a different taste or aesthetic being forced to live with something designed without their consent. Therefor, we may develop and even more advanced form of mutable architecture that can reconfigure itself on occasion to keep the landscape more alive and interesting. We have already achieved this in many places where buildings move and change shapes or use elaborate display systems to change color or show new content on the sides. One Korean building even has gone so far as to make itself invisible by projecting an image on each side of what it would look like if it weren't there. There are also new metamaterials that have the same effect by channeling light around themselves.

Having lived in Santa Fe, New Mexico for 8 years, I became very fond of the adobe buildings and the way they blended into the surrounding landscape, producing a harmonious coexistence.

The color palettes provided by nature seem most pleasing and I would imagine they should be in ample use in the future.

Gardens and Parks

Beautiful gardens and parks take an enormous amount of work to create and maintain yet they remain some of our favorite places to spend time. It's no surprise that large gardens are associated with royalty and wealth. Only they could afford the land and the staff of full-time gardeners and landscapers to maintain them. In the Cosmic Age, many gorgeous public spaces could be created and maintained all year round by human volunteers who enjoyed gardening, assisted by robots who could do the hard labor with not so much as a single complaint. Because the air would be clean, the fragrances of the flowers would also add to the delight.

Nature Parks would remain essential links between wilderness and people, providing trails, campgrounds and controlled access that protected the species of the park. Keeping it clean and maintained could be somewhat automated and sentries could help prevent unnatural forest fires.

Schools

Because Mental Wealth would overtake Material Wealth as a more primary goal in life, the role of education and schools would become even more elevated. State-of-the-art schools could be found in any neighborhood and long gone would be the days of good schools for the privileged few. More emphasis could be placed on higher matters and less so preparing students for a life of mundane work for pay, encouraging creativity, social studies and philosophical thought. Those that were interested could follow political or technical interests or any number of focused interests.

Schools will be a place to elevate our thinking, focus on our roles in society and to develop skills we can enjoy for life. The pressure of grades and scholastic testing will be deemphasized naturally. One simply moves on when one is ready for the path one has chosen. There will be no time in life when one couldn't take a free class on some topic of interest. We may see certain schools where classes are populated by many age groups instead of monolithic blocks of students of the same age.

Primary school at first would be more dedicated to the inner life of the child, letting them explore social connections and play. Language and other skills will be much more easily learned with a myriad of assistive devices and tutors. There will always be an incentive to learn because one can get more out of life that way and as new forms of "social capital" become more important than one's salary, those with more mental wealth will be happier and have more potential in life.

Travel Pathways

The switch to electromagnetic, automated transportation offers a chance to reimagine road systems. Smart roads need not be Nature killing dead zones but can themselves be solar collectors. Magnetic levitation would be possible with the advent of high temperature superconductors. Flying vehicles would abound and so the skyways would need to be highly managed to avoid chaos. The flow of traffic would be regulated similar to how Internet traffic is now controlled, efficiently coordinating high speed transport and intersections. Instead of delivering data packets, these systems will deliver people and the time spent traveling will not be wasted because one will not be as limited to what one can do during transit.

Rail and Hyperloop[25] tunnel systems could make inter and intra-city travel speedy and safe without disrupting Nature or the landscape. Hyperloops can even be constructed multi-level to increase throughput.

Air travel would also be electromagnetic, possible running on compact fusion systems. Hypersonic air travel could connect distant parts of the Earth in ways we can barely appreciate. New generations of space faring vehicles could make traveling 200 miles straight up as

---

[25] https://en.wikipedia.org/wiki/Hyperloop

commonplace as going on a Sunday drive, changing our relationship to space and ushering in a new type of habitat in orbits around the Earth and Moon and even other planets.

If something as revolutionary as anti-gravity is discovered, then everything would change and our ideas of what's possible today would be come very antiquated including all notions of roads and other systems built to handle heavy loads since these loads would presumably become much less if anything.

Food

Food, perhaps the most delightful and primal of needs. We all love and need food. There are five important aspects when thinking about food:

Taste
Nutrition
Ethical sourcing
Preparation
Presentation

Food, and ingestion in general, is the closest thing we have to a time machine. By eating food and drinking water and intaking air, we give ourselves more physical time, or at least make a withdrawal from our *Time Account*. Likewise by lacking these or eating or breathing the wrong things, we give ourselves less physical time, poison being a quick way to die. The optimal food tastes great, is highly nutritious, ethically sourced and prepared and presented beautifully. These are not hard to achieve and as mentioned above, one can use the same amount of time and the same ingredients to produce terrible food or good food.

The means of food production in the future can be expected to be much different, whether by the changes in farming, new food substances or ways of presenting food. If the food satisfies all of the criteria above, then it can be said to be good food. If everybody has ready access to good food, the world will be a much better place than it is today.

If you are a meat lover, you know well that the treatment of animals is not always as it should be. I expect the use of animals as a source of food to dwindle for two reasons:

There will be more delicious substitutes

Current methods don't follow the laws of Sustainability, especially with a growing population to feed. Detroit alone eats 27,000 chickens per hour and the US eats over 8 Billion chickens per year, more than all the people on Earth!

There is absolutely nothing that prevents us from creating even more fantastic meat substitutes and we already have delicious vegetarian foods so there is no reason to lament the demise of animal husbandry, a form of torture in human terms.

Unlike the other animals that eat each other in the Natural World, we have developed compassion and empathy and understand suffering. Our higher mind struggles with our inner beast and the inner beat mostly wins. But we can overcome this and rise to a true level of stewardship if we can remove ourselves from this cruel cycle.

Animals

Animals are co-inhabitants of the Earth. We all share the same Tree of Life. Like us, they feel pain, enjoy moving about and many creatures have obvious close bonds with each other. We ourselves have enjoyed the company of pet animals for millennia and even attribute nobility and higher characteristics such as a dog's unconditional love or a cat's calm, regal pose. Animals have lots to teach us and have very special skills and abilities we lack. They operate on a level more in tune with Nature.

As such, it is important that animals be given Rights and that we use our special gifts to protect and preserve them and their habitats as though they were a part of our Human family. They are, and a world lacking in animal diversity has lost a huge part of its Natural Physical Wealth.

Because of our prowess with genetics, it would not be even shocking for us to be able to essentially have the lion lay down with the lamb in the future, basically creating more compatibility between the creatures of Earth and so the notion of certain compatible animals sharing spaces with humans could be expanded and add to the enjoyment of life.

Animal Pathways

Currently, we build with little or no regard for the needs of animals and their migratory paths. With very little effort on our part, we can incorporate safe passageways for animals connecting contiguous wilderness areas. This holistic approach to Nature will improve our well-being and make the Earth a friendlier place for all of its inhabitants. An added benefit is instead of having to drive out of the city to find wilderness, one could enter directly through designated portals and take Nature walks right in the city, perhaps using some protective assistance where needed.

Garbage and Waste

All processes produce waste. It's a part of the bargain of life and entropy guarantees it. In the Cosmic Age, not only will there be far less waste but the waste that is produced will be much more easily recycled with automation and nanotechnology reclaiming the raw materials to be used again and again. Organic waste can be used in various beneficial ways as fertilizers, compost and mulch for the parks and gardens and landscapes, creating a sustainable cycle. Long gone will be the days of burying a mishmosh of toxic items in large landfills. Some types of waste can be sent to pyrolytic converters where they are burned at such extreme temperatures they are broken into the primary elements of the periodic table, perfect for nanotechnology.

Energy Production

All of this automation and activity will require lots of clean Energy to operate. Fortunately, energy is one of the most abundant of the Cosmic Resources. However, as we have learned with Climate

Change and Global Warming, the Earth's biosphere is a *closed system*. Therefor we will need to operate well within the the natural balance that the Earth has developed. The First Law of Thermodynamics states that energy cannot be created or destroyed in a closed system. This is fundamental to understanding the delicate balance between the oceans, the atmosphere and biological entities that inhabit the Earth. This homeostasis or equilibrium must be maintained to obey the rule of Sustainability. Each source of energy must be carefully considered for its long-term impact. Take Geothermal, for example. If we were to continually harvest heat from the core of the Earth we may run a danger of cooling it to a point where the Iron stops moving sufficiently to weaken the electromagnetic shield that protects us from the Solar Wind. We have seen what happens when we harvest fossilized sunlight in the form of oil and coal, adding yesteryear's energy input from the Sun to today's input.

As a rule of thumb, we should try to stay roughly in the same range of what the Sun provides us since this is what the Earth evolved to use. In fact, we must also be mindful that the Earth never used all of the energy it received but bounced a large portion of it back into space and locked other parts of it into organic molecules through photosynthesis. The first order of business is to create an Energy Budget and stay within that down here on Earth. Space is another matter and we would then be creating many, many smaller closed systems, each one with its own limits and needs.

Energy storage is a huge key to successful and sustainable energy usage. New types of batteries and capacitors will be able to handle this and energy can be then distributed in a far less centralized fashion.

In addition, clean nuclear Fusion can be used to generate massive amounts of electrical energy by mimicking the same process that powers the Sun[26].

The efficiency of robots and computers will play a large role in how much energy is required. Some robots could conserve energy by moving slowly such as ocean cleanup devices and go about their tasks 24 hours per day, eventually getting to a maintenance level.

All means of energy production, distribution and maintenance can be performed by auxons and therefore have no costs associated.

Privacy

By removing the incentives to profitize personal information, it would become much less in demand. Nevertheless, we already have begun the process of securing private information in a decentralized blockchain system where one's medical and other records are kept safely and requesters of this information, clients, could only ask for very specific parts of it with a temporary entitlement key. The inventor of HTML, Tim Berners Lee has made it his life's mission to change the way privacy is handled, giving the power back to the individual.

This becomes even more important in an automated society where facial recognition and other such tracking are nearly flawless and you location and activities can be recorded. It is paramount

---

[26] https://www.lockheedmartin.com/en-us/products/compact-fusion.html

that this information is ONLY used anonymously or in the service of you, the individual, and not for nefarious reasons.

On top of this, nanotechnology enables the creation of "bugs" to spy on people that were invisible even in a microscope. This would make it very hard for criminals and terrorists to plot attacks, if they wanted to but also raises ethical issues that would need to be controlled from the gOS Core Immutable Privacy Policy.

Defense Systems

Even in a perfect society, there will need to be defenses against the unknown, the criminal, the insane and malevolent actors. There will also need to be safeguards against accidents, natural disasters and basically, the forces of entropy. I see these as falling into five main categories:

Military: Defense against external threats

Law Enforcement: Defense against internal threats

Investigation: Fact finding and forensics

Fire Protection: Defense against all fire types

Emergency Services: Handlers for medical emergencies and disasters

Ideally, the military component would not be needed but if there were competing systems walled off from each other or the non participants were of a militant nature, it would be required.

Because the physical world will always have entropy, there will always be crime and accidents. Therefor, law enforcement and investigation will be needed, though at a much lower level than we have now since much crime is in pursuit of material things which would be obviated in the Cosmic Age. Forest fires could still be accidentally sparked and nature will still shock and awe with hurricanes, floods, tornadoes and such.

I will intentionally omit any ideas I may or may not have for advanced weapons as my desire to share my good thoughts eclipse my desire to give people more ideas for ways to harm one another. I will say that the most powerful weapon will always be information, communication and the mind itself.

Crime and Punishment

The nature of what is considered a crime and how society chooses to mete out punishment changes drastically from time to time and place to place. In a certain way, our own homes are a microcosm of this system. At one point it was a truism, "Spare the rod, spoil the child," and corporal punishment was not only considered normal but required. As psychology developed, more was understood about the fallacy of this method of "teaching," often teaching the child the exact opposite of the desired lesson and that humans were really just physical beasts to be beaten into submission. It's an oversimplification, but essentially much of our system of punishment is built on the same principle—those in power physically control the offender in a way that is not pleasant.

Not surprisingly, the rates of recidivism in such systems is quite high and those that have adapted more rehabilitative approaches much less so, such as certain European countries have done.

Many types of crimes derive from things that will be ostensibly eliminated and greatly reduced in the Cosmic Age including:

Poverty and desperation

Mental disturbance

Greed for material things

Lust for power

Even so, it would seem impossible, given the complexities of human interactions, to every fully eliminate all of the causes of crime. But we could reduce the chances of such to nominal levels by eliminating poverty and increasing mental wealth and health and having better ways of detecting problems before they grew out of hand.

Most crimes could be punished by a rehabilitative approach and including social service. It would be hard to imaging a form of criminal that either couldn't be fixed if there were a defective mental function or made into a better person through proper guidance.

Punishment of Robots and Virtual Punishment

It is not unreasonable to assume that as droids and robots more closely mimic their creators they could also get caught up in criminal activity. If robotic entities are never proven to be sentient or better, proven to be non-sentient then it would make no sense to punish them and they could be fixed or recycled as defective equipment. However, if they *were* sentient and could learn a new behavior then the analog of rehabilitation would be reprogramming.

We have no idea what sort of temporal frame such being operate in (i.e. how time passes) and it's possible that they could experience billions of years in one of our years or perhaps this sense would be programmable itself. It would be inhumane and cruel to program them to suffer no matter the duration but we would have the awesome responsibility not to create our own synthetic eternal damnation. If Kurzweil is correct and we can upload our own consciousness to a device, this becomes even more important.

Crimes Against Robots

In the TV series of Westworld, an elaborate amusement park is created, filled with lifelike Old West androids which are to be generally criminally abused at will by the somewhat sociopathic human participants. They are shot, raped, knifed and otherwise killed without penalty and are simply rebooted and erased for the next shift. This illustrates a dehumanization of machines, even when they are perfectly human looking and acting. More than dehumanization, this is debiofication, not even allowing to consider these a form of life whatsoever. This particular use of robots is no different in spirit than what is commonly done in video games only that the virtual character is now a material character.

Sabotage is another form of crime that could be common where elaborate devices are caused to malfunction or are ruined by angry, insane or threatened people. In the Cosmic Age, these devices will belong to society so it would be normal to categorize such crimes of sabotage as defacing of public property, except in cases of self-defense which could arise. Some devices could be vital to the well-being of thousands of people say in directing fast-moving traffic or delivering food or passengers and thus could carry higher penalties. Naturally, there will be defenses in place and getting away with such crimes could be difficult. These crimes would be similar to willfully destroying infrastructure or public transportation today, with one caveat, there is no cost to replace the device, other than the time it takes to do so. However, if people were killed or hurt or such was attempted in the act, the crime would be elevated accordingly.

If advanced robots are proven at some point to be sentient, then a new set of ethics would arise to protect them as we would ourselves or animals and Robot Rights would be required.

Guns and Weapons

The ability to kill another person in self-defense is so built into the human psyche that it was put into the US Constitution as a Right. However, at the time of writing, the only guns that existed were muskets and they were notorious for slow loading, inaccuracy and fired one shot at a time. Many technical strides evolved the gun to its modern form and they are far more deadly now, therefore it is easier to kill someone or even many people at once than ever.

We have placed restrictions on certain types of weapons in the general population as deemed necessary for the safety of society such as bombs, cannons, machine guns and the like. However, at times, the laws get behind the "right to bear arms" and we experience extreme violence as a result. Much of this is due not to the weapon itself, but the mental poverty of the shooter, which will be greatly reduced in the Cosmic Age.

Another form of shooting is for recreational purposes such as target shooting.

If we were to continue evolving guns as we have, then we could see far more deadly versions with smart bullets that could shoot around corners of from miles away and never miss their targets. Of course it would be preposterous to say that all future weapons must be allowed because it is our right and there will indeed be more restrictions as time goes by. However, there will be folks who enjoy the activity of shooting traditional firearms and there should be no need to restrict this so long as safety measures are taken.

That being said, non-lethal forms of self-defense could be every bit as effective for the purpose of disabling an assailant and target practice could easily be simulated virtually or by electronic means and the actual use of lead projectiles would be obsolete for the enjoyment of the sport.

Unfortunately, the notion of defense against tyranny using firearms is already quaint given the mismatch of power between civilian and military weapons and this would become geometrically more lopsided against an AI-driven or robotic military that one couldn't even really kill. So the best defense against abuse of power will always be Mental Wealth and Democracy and the proper oversight of the military for and by the People.

One can expect highly sophisticated detection systems in the future that can prevent all manner of weapons from being used in the wrong way or the wrong place.

Robots and Droids

Since we know that there will be a lot of robots in the future, it's important to understand them well. Some robots are sort of disturbing to watch, especially the ones that mimic the human form. Robots can be stationary. Robots can be divided into two main categories:

Utility Bots: Those that perform specific functions such as we see in auto factories. These include automated transport systems, entertainment systems and cleaning bots with important subtypes:

> **Minibots**: Those that are toy-sized and are capable of flight and getting into small spaces.

> **Microbots:** Those that are quite small, like small insects. These can be used as sentries and sensors without raising much notice. These can fly.

> **Nanobots**: Those that are invisible to the naked eye and perform actions on a microscopic scale. These can be airborne.

> **Proxybots**: These devices represent the telepresence of an individual or a group of people sharing a location in space and time and transmit data back to the receivers.

Droids: Those that roughly or exactly mimic humans and animals and generally created to interact with humans.

> **Androids**: Those designed to mimic humans in appearance and manner. These apply to any animal form. (eg. Data from Star Trek)

> **Techdroids**: Those that are styled as technology but interact in similar or stylized ways. (eg. C3PO, R2D2)

Robots Building Robots

When robots build other robots or even build more of themselves, these made robots are said to be *Auxons*. It is only through the use of auxons that the Cosmic Systems can scale up to the required levels. Large-scale structures in space or governing the chain of production from extraction to delivery of finished goods requires the automation itself to be automated. Mathematically speaking, this recursive system must be incomplete[27] and requires a Master Creator at the top of the chain, governing the rules of operation and the purpose of the automation. Much of this would eventually be handled by the gOS which itself is governed by humans, democratically.

Of course, since we get to govern the design of robots there is no particular limit on how they will look, how smoothly or quickly they will operate, etc. I would only say that public facing robots

---

[27] https://en.wikipedia.org/wiki/Gödel%27s_incompleteness_theorems

should be made safe, aesthetically pleasing, generally quiet and with the sole purpose to serve life and improve it. Up until the point where we can confirm that a robot is actually conscious and can experience pain they are not to be considered citizens of the society even though they may mimic one very well. If at a point they were declared and verified conscious (we can't even do that for ourselves), they would possibly gain new rights but that would create a possible avenue of extinction for humans. If Kurzweil is correct and we could at some point upload ourselves into these machines then we may face another conundrum of how many copies of ourselves we are allowed to make and whether each copy is conferred the same rights, if any at all.

There have been thoughtful books written on Robot Rights[28] and the movie *AI* makes us feel very uneasy and delve into our darkest corners of thought, the ones that produced slavery as a means of material satisfaction, so it's not going to be easy to figure out the right course. In essence, we are moving to create a class of robot "slaves," not only subhumans, but sub-life. Unlike human slaves, these slaves could be theoretically programmed to have no free will or even to feel happiness and reward in serving it's human masters, if such a thing were possible. We will always have a tendency to anthropomorphize entities that mimic us, even though at the very core of that entity is darkness and no provable sense of *being*.

That is not to say that we shouldn't *love* these robots and treat them with respect. Step out a level for a moment and perhaps even adapt a Native American spiritual belief that *all* matter is alive (Animism) and imbued with a magical force from the Great Spirit. I rather like this attitude toward the world because it allows everything to be included in the Eternal Dance we call life. And recall, the Cosmos is the provider of these robots and the Cosmic Products so in a very real sense, they are alive as extensions of ourselves and our ancestors. To have a love and appreciation for the inanimate, unconscious things in the world enriches the experience of living and makes it more grand. Something as simple as a rock, upon closer and closer examination, is teeming with a miraculous mini cosmos filled with atoms and all manner of molecules, swarming electrons, photons and subatomic particles and God knows what else. It does us no harm to appreciate these things.

Then there are the Hybrids, the cyborgs who are part bio and part machine. This form has so many variations it would be hard to list them all but here are some of the main possibilities:

Augmented Intelligence: Where some device is interfaced with our brains and our senses that could extend our cognitive abilities or extend our sensory capabilities. We already have Augmented Reality systems that can provide us information in an overlay of what we see and hear. With Virtual Reality, these would be used in conjunction with Proxybots to experience telepresence. Potentially, these interfaces would be so powerful as to afford 2-way communication with software that could both be controlled directly by the mind and also directly "beam" thoughts into our minds as though they were real.

Exo Gear: Equipment we can wear or get into and become stronger, faster or more suited to a task such as firefighting or lifting heavy things.

Prosthetics: Replacements or extensions of limbs or organs.

---

[28] https://mitpress.mit.edu/books/robot-rights

Large Automated Systems and Megabots

By working in coordination and tandem, unlimited robot subsystems can be connected into what is essentially a large Megabot that performs a complex function on a larger scale. In such systems each subtask would be handled by one section and passed to the next as an input for its function until the finished work product or result was produced. Such systems could be used for sorting garbage and producing recyclable materials, running factories or transportation systems. Such systems would be required to enable the advantages of the Cosmic Age.

Virtualization and Proxies

Virtual Reality (VR), Augmented Reality (AR) and Telepresence (TP) will all play a major role in every aspect of life in the future. If quantum entanglement can ever be harnessed as a communication medium, we could be present at any place in the Universe in Real-time. Even with the speed of light as the limit, the range of telepresence could be astonishing. I envision remote sensors so sophisticated that they can transmit a 3-D presence to someone from all manner of perspectives from that of a bug on a tree or the ground, to a cell in the body, transmitting not only visible light but other information as well. Telepresence is already in use and many ways from remote therapy sessions to telecommuting. It's a great time saver and could continue to give us a great bounty of time spent on more important, rewarding things.

Used in schools, children in remote areas could attend classes anywhere on Earth and intercultural exchanges will be commonplace. One can expect to see a proliferation of Proxy bots in classrooms of many types, perhaps using avatar-like skins or android styling or could be down and dirty utility devices with 360 cameras and audio. Virtual Reality can be used to create a Historical Time Machine where students not only read about history but can join in or entirely fantastical and imaginary worlds can be created to explore. There are no limits to the kinds of training one could participate in virtually and in fact develop mastery.

Of course, entertainment will be one of the primary uses of virtualization, and we already have many such games, movies and art installations so they will only grow in complexity and richness. However, because of the way we've evolved, this technology can also easily terrify as well and it is in fact quite dangerous in the wrong hands.

There is a huge potential for therapeutic uses of AR and VR where users can train their minds to be calm or overcome phobias.

Star Trek perhaps had the coolest implementation of virtualization, the famed *Holodeck*. A Holodeck requires no special equipment on the user but instead creates a fully simulated environment, within the bounds of the Holodeck.

Taken one step further, it is not at all preposterous to have thoughts beamed directly into the mind in which case full dream-like experiences could be had including all sensations of touch, pleasure, pain, smell, etc. could be experienced.

Extended Intelligence

We are only at the beginning stages of AI and Machine Learning and it's already one of the most important developments in history. As stated above, it is expected to increase in power and possibly exponentially so. Regardless of how it happens or how extensive it becomes, it will always be an extension of human intelligence and we will forever remain the ancestors of what we created.

However, at the point where we are unable to "keep up" which is pretty much as of writing this treatise, we are in danger of losing control of our creation, not unlike Dr. Frankenstein. When AI is allowed to turn upon itself and rapidly improve itself, we can expect the unexpected. Therefore, it would be highly advisable to proceed with a set of guidelines:

The final control over the top level of AI must remain with humans.

AI must be always programmed with high ethical intent with the *sole* purpose of improving life for humans and animals and the Earth.

AI programming should always be carried out with specific, fairly narrow *objectives* in mind. Objective-oriented programming (not to be confused with object-oriented) would be safe so long as the objectives were carefully considered and not open-ended, vague or to large in scope such as: make a being that can become our overlord or make everybody happy or rid the world of its problems.

We must have in place contingency plans for rogue AI.

It's not even clear that these objectives are possible given that the intelligence we could unleash may far exceed our own on every level and we could simply be outsmarted by it, like playing checkers against a 4-D Chess master. We could become ants and mental midgets in the aegis of a hyper-intelligence. So to whatever degree is possible, we need to plan ways we can remain in final control.

It's probably not necessary for us to create such an intelligence in the first place. So the safest thing may to be more objective-oriented and concentrate on specific objectives we would like to achieve with Extended Intelligence and not dive into the deep waters of self-improving intelligence more than needed, just to satisfy our curiosity. An ounce of prevention may in this case be equal to infinity pounds of cure. By so doing, we could remain the directors and not become the directed

Laziness and Apathy

People tend to take the path of least resistance. This is one of the tenants of Game Theory. One of the dystopian models of society has the masses caught up in Virtual Reality games and experiences, losing interest in the Real World, basically becoming themselves a mere pointless extension of a machine intelligence. These people are not much different from the Lotus Eaters (λωτοφάγοι) encountered by Odysseus on his journeys. It was not easy for Odysseus and his sailors to extricate themselves from this island because the delicious plant had the effect of making them not care about getting home. It may be that this behavior would be looked at as a form of addiction and thus the "drug" of Virtual Reality would need to be regulated and somehow limited to protect the dignity of life and to encourage a higher life of usefulness in society and admiration for Nature. One the other hand, entertainment, relaxation and fun should always be an important part of living so a balance should be sought.

Besides this virtual lotus plant, we would expect any number of actual drugs that could produce similar apathy and satisfaction. In present society we see a scourge of opioid addiction that causes people to lose all care of consequences and become powerless to escape the grip of the drug. Antidotes would be required to match the power of such drugs.

Medical Science

One of the great benefits of the Cosmic Age is the level of understanding of biological processes and the conditions that cause disease. We can expect to leave behind the ridiculous days where it was thought unprofitable to cure a madady rather than string someone out on a lifetime prescription. Every aspect of medical technology will improve including:

> Early detection of problems
> Treatments of bacterial and viral infections
> Elimination of cancer and heart disease
> Cures for genetic disorders including those that are degenerative
> Minimally invasive surgery
> Repair of disfiguration, limbs, organs, bones and tissue
> Spinal and central nervous system repairs
> Highly improved nutrition and promotion of wellness
> Mental wellness

The administering of healthcare should always include humans, compassion and preserve the dignity of the sick. One would anticipate a fair number of assistive and automated processes to be able to carry out all of the tasks. The notion of hospitals as we know them may become obsolete and emergency care could be administered on-site and remotely in many cases. Even complex surgeries could be performed using mobile surgical units.

It is obvious that even some of the medical jobs requiring the most knowledge and skills can be automated.

Non Participants

Human freedom requires free will and choice to live as we wish so long as it doesn't interfere with the freedom or well-being of others. Not everybody and perhaps even quite significant portions of humanity would desire to live outside of this Cosmic System even in all of its grandeur and advantages, for example the Amish people who eschew all technology for religious reasons. In general, I see no problem with setting aside areas of the Earth that are allowed to operate as they always have or in support of a purist humanism. This would be a choice on how they spend *their* time. In fact, there is something very compelling about such a simplicity and it may be that this is our final destination anyway and what everybody truly wants, a simple happy life. So we should always seek to learn about our true nature and the meaning of life and not automatically and mindlessly become the erudite people of Laputa from Swift's *Gulliver's Travels* who lived in a castle in the sky removed from the real world. Non participation may be the ultimate participation in Life. We don't know yet.

It would likely be a popular travel destination to go to places where the simple life was lived.

Dependency and Upgrades

Because we would rely on properly functioning automation for our daily needs, it would be wise to design systems, to the degree possible, so that no one failure could cascade to bring down or damage other systems. The programming principles of Encapsulation and Modularity should be adhered to in which very succinct areas of functionality are encapsulated to expect certain inputs and produce required outputs and be swappable for a similar or upgraded system. Upkeep and upgrades could be performed regularly with such techniques. Critical Systems would also employ redundancy where required so that operations could continue while failed systems were being replaced.

There should be much practice of crafts and growing of food and other legacy skills so that people could regularly experience those things that connect us to the Earth and our ancestors. This may even be a social requirement and on certain days of the year, automation would be reduced or opted off to enable a simpler form of living. Out of these practices could come more sustained periods of simpler and less dependent living.

Room for Funkiness and Vintage

For many, including myself, having lived in New York City, a certain pleasure and comfort comes from the chaos and disorder and messiness. I think certain places should maintain a more organic and soulful vibe I refer to as *funkiness*. Utopia needn't mean antiseptic or perfectly clean and orderly and it certainly doesn't mean that for many people. Nevertheless, there were many parts about life in the city that were absurd such as homeless guys trying to wipe your car window with a greasy rag on every corner or disgusting piles of rotting garbage in black plastic bags during garbage strikes. New York was a lot cooler when more people could afford to live there, attracting interesting people who created art and wrote poems and made films. It has since been "gentrified" and "Disneyfied" and has lost most of that edge and become safe for business. So in the Cosmic Age we can have cities that artists can afford to live in because cost is eliminated from the formula. The cities can simply operate better, corruption free yet maintain their character and new cities can also arise with a different vibe.

Smaller towns to this day have kept many dirt roads in place, not always for saving money but because of the added rustic charm they provide, not to mention they are more Natural and thus superior in that way.

We have created so much material that will and always has become the source of collection and keeping for its beauty, historical connections and rarity. Certain skills and methods are lost from generation to generation, era to era and so those things made thusly become rare and valued more. Ironically, the nanotechnology of the future will be able to create faithful reproductions on an atomic level, but the originals will always be more prized. Because of the configurability of matter, entire towns could switch into "vintage mode" of any era, adding to the delight and appreciation of history.

Religion and Worship

On this topic there may never be total agreement and it remains a personal choice. However, *logic tells us* that not all religions can be right at the same time so either all but one, or all, are off the mark of reality, each one thinking *they* are the true religion. Fortunately, there are common threads of morality and wisdom between most religions that we can agree on. As to places of worship both in location and quantity, this will need to be debated since stewardship is the main criterion of property management in the Cosmic Age. With configurable architecture, it would be easier to create multi-purpose houses of worship instead of filling the landscape with different churches, synagogues, mosques and temples. Legacy architecture could be under special protection to preserve the historical record and magnificent structures could be created in Space where the Firmament could be contemplated in a more direct and enlightened way.

For religious reasons, some days of the week may require taking a break from the electromagnetic, solar-powered assistive systems that would abound and so walking and other forms of abstinence would be available much as they are today.

The Government would remain strictly separated from Religion up until the point where an actual Deity directly commanded us otherwise in a way that was clearly understood and not subject to myriad interpretations. Until that point, which would probably never come since Deities, if they exist, seem to use an Invisible Hand approach, it would be treated as a personal matter and not one requiring the state to intervene other than to protect Rights that didn't contradict the Rights of others, somewhat as it is today.

A sufficiently advanced civilization could create the effects of Deity to the point where relative to us, they *are* Deities so it might not be easy to determine the difference between a Metaphysical Being and a Physical Being that is orders of magnitude more advanced than us, but it might not matter in that case. In either case we have no clear, agreed upon modern evidence of such beings. This could be likened to a Modern person landing a flying car in ancient Egypt or Greece with lasers and projectors and computers where they would likely be worshipped.

Fame and Reward

Even if we reached a place in history where basically everybody was wealthy, beautiful and had some gift or another, unless we became completely homogeneous, we'd presumably still have outstanding individuals in one way or another. Of course, if we were only a horde of clones, no one would stand out and the idea of fame would seem silly other than some form of lottery for your "15 minutes of fame." Also, we may outgrow the whole notion of fame, not even placing value on it. I would conjecture, as long as there is chaos in the world, there will be both fame and infamy (negative fame). There will be individuals who by whatever circumstances, are more inspired, harder working or more dedicated than others. There will also be individuals who are more misguided, depraved or craven than others. So likely the notion of fame and legend will continue well into the future because every story needs protagonists and antagonists to keep our interest.

In the Communist Soviet Union, where every comrade received the exact same base salary, star individuals would receive perks in the form of more money or better living quarters, better food, often not insignificant. However, the State could arbitrarily pick someone out and turn them into a ballerina by stealing them from their family at a young age and training them 10 hours a day for their childhood so it wasn't necessarily a natural process. In such a system, one could also become more powerful and famous by being more ruthless which is a little closer to classic Darwinian selection. Let's not forget this was a failed experiment, though with external forces working against it too. The forces of greed and corruption were not eliminated and so the system failed, though it produced invaluable insights into communal living that historians are still trying to understand.

But in a society where money doesn't exist and a diamond bracelet is just another free doodad created by auxons, how would we reward outstanding individuals or would we even do it? It goes against our evolutionary nature not to reward the most fit among us. Animals fight to become dominant and garner breeding rights. Would we retain this primal instinct?

The notion of not having outstanding individuals rubs the American psyche wrong (I can't speak for other cultures). We have built our culture around the merits and importance of the individual. Yet to be famous is to accept the premise that one is somehow deserving of the fame and superior to others in the agreed amount of one's fame, which on the face of it is egotistical. There are plenty of examples of famous folks displaying humility and the altruistic desire to use this fame for the betterment of society. However, upon examination, fame also requires a large dose of luck. We've heard famous people say, "I got my lucky break when…" A lot of lucky things have to happen for one to become famous, regardless of how hard one worked to get there. Good genetics, good parents, meeting the right people at the right time, etc. We certainly know there are many extremely talented folks who never achieve fame.

This is why I list Fame as an asset of Material Wealth—its value is also somewhat imaginary and arbitrary. Therefor, it is likely that the superficial aspect of fame would be devalued at some point and so to seek fame would be to seek something with no intrinsic value. To acquire fame without seeking it is a different matter, somewhat out of one's control—for better or worse.

I remain conflicted about this. I look at a musical band like the Beatles, four working class lads from Liverpool, who worked their tails off at their craft and were given a musical gift that touched billions of people and that can't be explained away easily. I personally believe they possessed a form of Spiritual Wealth that manifested itself through music and inspiration, almost a type of Divinity. Yet, John Lennon, for all his fame, ended up in a plain white apartment in New York and was at his happiest as a father to his child, cooking meals and playing his white piano so his material rewards were not so extreme as far less important or talented famous or wealthy people, perhaps an important lesson.

Acknowledgement is a form of love. Every child needs encouragement and so do adults. So no matter what we decide is a proper reward for outstanding achievements in a particular field, it would be unloving and wrong not to properly acknowledge it. Entry into a Hall of Fame is one such reward, creating a permanent memorialization of the individual's contribution. Louise Borges would probably have written a short story about the Infinite Hall of Fame. In this hall, far in the future, there are an infinite number of famous individuals. You enter the hall and you will never see anyone you've heard of and are simply presented with a random selection from infinity.

Who wins the Nobel Prize when a super-intelligent AI Agent (i.e. Watson on steroids) invents a brilliant new economic theory or materials breakthrough in Chemistry? The programmer? What if the program was written by another AI Agent? In a certain way, this illustrates how such prizes actually belong to everybody because without all that came before and great luck and fortune, no one could ever reach such an apex of intellectual prowess.

Competition

Is it human nature to compete? It would almost seem to be built in on a fundamental level and biological evolution is itself a form of competition for mating rights—the survival of the fittest. However, we are the only species that seems to have sports or Olympics where we crown winners and send losers packing outside of mating. Capitalism is built on such competition where the market determines winners and losers. Andrew Carnegie in his *Gospel of Wealth* claims that without this we would remain in the dark ages and only by rewarding the hardest working and most clever among us can we truly progress. To a degree, this is true, but only in a relative way. There is always someone faster, smarter, stronger or more ruthless that can assume power over perfectly worthy people. And so often those that get there first protect advantages and deter fair competition so his idealized market is easily corrupted to crush real competition.

In the end, one must define what it means to win. Also, one must determine what is worth competing over and why. So much competition is arbitrary and depends on so many external factors that we are measuring people based on things out of their control such as where they were born, like the fact that warm-climated countries don't generally fare well in Winter Sports.

Nothing in the Cosmic Age would deter athletic competition but certain sports that tend to create injuries would likely become obsolete because there would be no financial incentive to sacrifice one's body for the entertainment of others. It would be interesting to see what percentage of the population would pursue athletics purely out of the desire to participate but with no other need.

As for market competition, this would become completely obsolete because the notion of markets would disappear with monetary systems and abundant goods for free. In the Cosmic Age, we would be competing against ourselves to make ourselves better, to make better things and to outdo previous generations in the perfection of material existence, no longer trying to beat our fellow humans or animals so that we can dominate. Losing in this competition would be to leave the world in worse shape, to create an underclass or to become mentally impoverished and feckless like the Eloi race of the future in the *Time Machine*.

Multiple Systems

Given the human ego, there is no reason to assume all people will subscribe to any one system of material distribution no matter how good it is. We also have no real way of knowing how large or all-encompassing such a system will tend to be or whether it will have natural boundaries. Therefor, it would be feasible for different competing systems to arise, and some of them may not abide by the core principle that Cosmic Resources are to be shared by all, creating a conflict of interest and reverting to the same behavior that we sought to overcome.

It is also possible that such systems could be cooperative and even share many components. It is my belief that as a matter of efficiency, mathematics and physics, such systems would eventually coalesce into a single system yet preserve the cultural and local character of each zone as desired.

Threats to Reaching the Cosmic Age

There are unfortunately numerous threats to us ever reaching the Cosmic Age or at least greatly forstalling it. These are divided into two types:

Avoidable:

Nuclear armageddon

Biological agents or mutant epidemics

Nanotechnology run amok

Human experiments run amok

Population overrun

Climate or biosphere disaster

Ocean death

Destroyed water supplies

Toxins in the environment

Unbounded or overreaching AI ("Skynet")

Rogue AI that is directed will ill intent

Mass extinction

Unavoidable:

Large asteroid impact*

Supervolcanoes*

Rogue black holes

Cosmic events

Alien invasion (not so likely or it probably would have already happened)

*We could, if detected in time, take measures to divert asteroids or vent pressure from supervolcanoes

Level I Civilization

Nikolai Semenovich Kardashev, Russian astrophysicist, proposed a scale to measure civilizations. A Level 1 Civilization would have some degree of mastery over the Planet, including harnessing all energy reaching the planet and some control over weather and climate. The Cosmic Age would represent the beginning of this phase. We have already shown that we can affect climate by changing carbon levels in the atmosphere. It is not too much of a leap to then control more precisely these levels and also you use other methods to change weather patterns, perhaps diverting hurricanes or dissipating dangers from other types of storms. Rain control could be used to combat drought conditions and snuff out fires so the benefits could be huge. However, without fully understanding ecosystem impact, this would be more dangerous than useful.

A civilization that reached this level would be a position to explore the Cosmos and eventually evolve to a Level 2 Civilization, perhaps after a thousand or so years. Some changes would occur on a geometrical scale so it's hard to predict the time scales.

It should be noted, we have no current evidence that such civilizations exist or that it is possible to achieve such a level before self-destruction overtakes the species.

So Far In the Future We Become Ourselves

We know so little about how we became who we are that we could very well already be the result of an Eternal Process that produces an endless cycle of machines and biological creatures that make machines that make biological creatures, ad infinitum. In other words, this may already be the best of all possible worlds and we don't know it as we search for something better. If the world is in fact some sort of simulation (not likely), then it's hard to see how we would ever become the ones running our own simulation, somehow escaping our own already running simulation. As such, we must always be mindful of the end purpose of any of our personal and collective activities and what we hope to accomplish and whether it truly is an improvement or simply another level of illusion.

Appendix A: Current Entities and Companies that Could Play a Role in the Cosmic Age

Much of what I have gone over has its roots in current activities as of 2018. Some are non-profit organization and government and others are commercial businesses and schools.

Organizations

Council On Extended Intelligence: https://globalcxi.org

Technical Committee for Robot Ethics: http://www.ieee-ras.org/robot-ethics

Companies

Alphabet: https://abc.xyz   (Google)

Apple: http://www.apple.com

IBM: http://www.ibm.com

Intel: http://www.intel.com

Microsoft: http://www.microsoft.com

Amazon: http://www.amazon.com

Lockheed Martin: https://www.lockheedmartin.com/en-us/index.html

Boeing: http://www.boeing.com

Airbus: http://www.airbus.com

Boston Dynamics: https://www.bostondynamics.com

Schools

MIT: http://www.mit.edu

St. John's College: http://www.sjc.edu

Stanford University: http://www.stanford.edu

Harvard: http://www.harvard.edu

Princeton: http://www.princeton.edu

Knowing the problems is fairly easy—one need only look around, read the news, read some books and try to raise a family in this world. But how do we feel about these things?

Appendix B: Simple Surveys

To discover an honest psychological context for this work, it would be very interesting to conduct a couple of Yes/No surveys to find out how people felt about either positive or negative changes with regard to these these conditions, using seemingly preposterous, yet pertinent, questions:

Survey One: A Great World

Would it bother you if everybody on Earth lived in a clean, safe place they liked?

Would it bother you if life in the ocean was allowed to replenish and forests were allowed to grow back in more places?

Would it bother you if everybody was wealthy and the conditions in 1 and 2 were also true?

Would it bother you to not have to work unless you enjoyed your work?

Would it bother you if the world population stabilized at a sustainable, comfortable level?

Would it bother you if you could rest and relax any time you needed to on your own schedule?

Would it bother you if you were never depressed and felt safe, secure, loved and happy?

Would it bother you if you had unlimited access to the best healthcare possible for no cost?

Survey Two: A Terrible World

Would it bother you if the Earth became a steaming hothouse with continuous large storms, drought and flood conditions and toxic waste was allowed to be dumped anywhere?

Would it bother you if all forests were cut down, most of the animals you know went extinct, Nature was paved over and mining and drilling had no limits?

Would it bother you if everybody lived in relative poverty except for a privileged few?

Would it bother you to have to work all of your life doing menial tasks for the privileged few so you could pay for basic things?

Would it bother you if the world population kept growing until the entire Earth was one big urban area?

Would it bother you if you could barely find time to rest and could rarely experience peace of mind?

Would it bother you if you were always depressed and felt great anxiety about your well-being?

Would it bother you if you could only gain access to healthcare if you weren't too sick and you had to work a significant portion of your life to afford basic healthcare?

If you answered Yes to any of the questions in the Survey One or No to any of the questions in the Survey Two, there may be something wrong with you and you should get that checked.

If you answered normally and honestly to Survey One then the natural thing is to think, of course, who wouldn't want these things, but that's all pie-in-the-sky fantasyland.

The Quick Read Version: For Those In a Hurry

Picture a world where poverty is nonsense and wealth as we know it is meaningless. This is a world free of garbage and pollution where people and animals live in harmony, cities are beautiful, Nature is revered and people spend their time in pursuit of interests and betterment, not chasing down a living. There are no banks, no taxes and money itself has been rendered pointless. Using available technology, this world is now well within reach with not significantly much more effort than we put into landing on the Moon but it will require great resolve and breaking very old habits and power structures—not easily done. The alternatives, current trends withstanding, are untenable, unsustainable and can lead to great sorrow and strife for all sentient life on Earth.

The thoughts and ideas behind this are written below but in essence the following will be shown:

There are **Three Domains of Accrual** within which we can accrue assets:

Physical

Educational

Metaphysical

There are five **Primary forms of Wealth** within these Domains of Accrual:

Physical wealth

Genetic wealth

Mental wealth

Spiritual wealth

Material wealth

Each Domain has special quantitative and qualitative assets, a corresponding poverty and debt, treasure, garbage and waste.

Wealth has four types of **Importance**:

Internal, for the possessor

External, as society sees it

Historical, as it affects history

Cosmic, as it affects the Cosmos, if at all

We all inherit **Foundational Cosmic Resources** for free:

Time: The Primary Resource

Space: The Secondary Resource

Energy: The Prime Mover

Matter: Crystalized Energy ($E = mc^2$)

Forces: Gravity, Electromagnetism, etc.

Quanta: The smallest blocks of Reality

Mathematics: The Universal Language of Order

Including **Practical Cosmic Resources**, also free of charge:

Sunlight, Wind, Ocean Tides, Molten Magma, Chemical and Nuclear Energy

Elements (eg. Oxygen, carbon, iron, silicon, gold, silver, etc.)

Molecular substances (eg. water, air, gems, etc.)

Biological resources (eg. Plants, animals, bacteria, oil, etc.)

Ore, geological resources containing elements we desire

Stars, planets, moons, asteroids, etc. (the results of Forces acting on Matter and Energy over Time in Space)

Crystals, a special form of molecules or elements

Undiscovered natural materials

In the future, via advanced, self-maintaining Automation and AI, involving no human labor, these resources can be turned into luxurious **Cosmic Products** of quality, beauty and usefulness, rendering notions of material wealth *obsolete*, including the concepts and mechanisms of money and monetary systems that rely on it.

With unlimited automated, and free, skilled labor in conjunction with free resources it becomes preposterous to charge for goods and services that the Cosmos provides.

I will show, as others have done, the roots of money and ownership to be imagined cultural constructs propped up by a generations-old story and pyramid scheme. I talk about the problems and complexities, many unnecessary, that we create and perpetuate through our belief in them.

A materially satisfied, post-scarcity world poses challenges to the purpose of life that only mental and spiritual enrichment can satisfy.

Time is the most valuable and the Primary Cosmic Resource. We profusely waste and steal it from each other through various schemes of business, scams, government and inefficiency.

Many ethical conundrums arise from a world without money and we are faced with questions about what we will do with our time, how will we work, or even *will we*, where we will live, the role of Nature, animals, etc.

The concept of extraterrestrial wealth and the general meaning of material wealth outside Earth makes little sense. This helps to illustrate the endgame of wealth.

Government will require an advanced Operating System, gOS, to manage the complexities and physical needs of a future, highly automated society.

The goal is a superior, sustainable life and society and to avoid extinction or self-destruction and to free humanity from the bonds of forced labor. The conclusion is that there is now nothing technically preposterous or unreasonable in solving nearly all of the problems that have plagued humanity for millennia.

When the Cosmic Provisional Systems are in place and the monetary system has become antiquated, we will have entered the **Cosmic Age,** a major step toward fulfilling our potential.